A SHINY NEW TOY

A SHINY
NEW TOY

— MARK LADO —

Published By Global Manufacturing Services

Published in the United States of America

ISBN (paperback): 978-1-7320475-3-2
ISBN (ebook): 978-1-7320475-4-9

ACKNOWLEDGEMENTS

I would like to thank Paul Kocak for being my writing coach. He has helped transform my writing from a mix of clunky tasks, textbook lessons, and emails to a modern novel style — well, generally in that direction. He once said something along the lines of, "People read for escape, drama, intrigue, entertainment, betrayal, evil, murder, or mayhem." This book has traces of these emotions with a few educational points scattered throughout.

I owe thanks to the following people for providing initial feedback in the early drafts: Peter Liao, Randy Pinto, Diane Hunter, and Andrew Chesterfield. Also, thanks to Sheila Milden for her creativity and editing, and Heather McCoy for the book cover design. Their insights were very helpful, resulting in significant improvements.

I can't thank my wife, Panjai Lado, enough for always supporting me and encouraging me to embark on this adventure. Finally, I am eternally grateful to my mom and dad, Shirley and Ron Lado, for too many things to list here.

–1–

HAPPY NOW? WHAT A MESS.

As the waiter took their order, Peter looked across the table and said with a sense of frustration, "We're losing business to our competitors. We are constantly rolling out new products, but our prices are at the high end."

Sarah smiled sweetly and reminded him, "You always say it's all about value not price."

Shaking his head, he replied, "And I still believe that. Many of our competitors' products have poor quality and appearance, a bad user interface, or a multitude of other issues."

"So what's the issue?" asked Sarah as she buttered her roll.

"Same as always, we missed a key customer product launch."

"Oh? Which product? Was it the commercial or residential unit with HEPA filters and ultraviolet light?"

"Unfortunately, both! Same technology just different parts."

"Oh, my lord. No wonder you can't sleep at night. Where do you think the problem lies?"

Pausing a moment, he pensively continued. "Well, I can't really blame Bob or Kevin even though they are the product managers. I can only blame myself. Somehow, I need to instill a culture at Pure Air that identifies risks and mitigates them. That should help develop the next generation of leaders who can work cohesively together. I think that's what the real problem is."

"Do you have the time and energy to do all that?"

"Honestly, no, I don't." With a small snort he continued, "But I know my team sure does. When I walk through the customer service office, people are just standing around chatting and it's like a bell goes off at 5 p.m.; the entire office is almost vacant by 5:02!"

Sarah took another sip of her Australian Cabsav. "Where do you think the passion went?"

"Well, it certainly didn't leave overnight, I suppose it took years and we just didn't see it slipping."

With concern in her voice, she asked, "Your management style has been the same over the years, right?"

He shrugged. "I think so, but I know I am not as positive as I used to be. I have very little patience and it shows in some meetings with me barking out orders." Peter took another sip of his Sazerac, calmed down, and said, "I have been trying, but maybe not in the right ways."

She reached across and placed her hand on his. "Dear, you have been very successful. But, times are changing. People want to invest their time with activities other than work. Maybe now it is time to move on and retire."

Peter sighed, "Maybe this is the year."

"Yeah, right." Sarah laughed. "You say that all the time but it hasn't happened yet."

Peter smiled and nodded in agreement. "I know. That said, I love you and will seriously think of a date, but I am certainly in no mood to talk about a party."

"I think you have just turned your sweet and savory Sazerac attitude into piss and vinegar. We have to celebrate and we will."

"On that note, I'm going to the bathroom."

Dinner arrived and Peter steered the conversation back to business. "I am at a crossroads with either retiring or turning Pure Air over to one of the executives. Neither path is very appealing right now."

Cutting into her meal, Sarah proclaimed, "Mmm, this prime rib is delicious. Peter, look at all you've accomplished. Are you expecting someone to be exactly like you?

He shook some salt and pepper onto his beef and vegetables. "No, but I believe the board of directors has lost confidence in my leadership. After the last board meeting, I heard they wanted to reinvigorate a discussion about succession planning."

"Hey, watch how much salt you are using! The doctor said it isn't good for you. But I agree with your concerns. I can tell the Pure Air's future is not as strong as it used to be."

He put the salt shaker down and said, "I think it is time I bring a consultant on board to shake things up, implement lean, effective practices, and develop the executives. I think that will help our staff adjust to a more competitive culture. I am certain we need outside influence to make this happen."

"Sounds like you have been thinking about this idea for a while and I agree, it is about time to make some changes. You just need to kick it off."

He looked worried. "This will be a culture change. I am not sure if any of us are ready for it."

Peter let out a slight sigh of resignation. "Ok. It's done. Time to make some changes."

—2—

MONDAY MISERY

J udgment Day arrives, as it does every Monday.

Fidgeting with the papers on the table, Anika, the director of customer service operations at Pure Air, let out a frustrated sigh. "It's 9 a.m. Where are Bob and Kevin? They're never here on time."

Anika has been with Pure Air for almost two years. On the other hand, Kevin has been with the firm for three years while Bob is a seasoned veteran with the company since the founding. Peter, the General Manager proudly talks about Anika, like she is some token object to be displayed on a shelf and admired. Her kryptonite was working with Bob and Kevin.

Anika didn't publish an agenda for the Monday business update meeting, but throughout the week she sent novel-length emails to Bob and Kevin with a copy to the staff stating her expectations. The emails highlighted many different problems. She would make a statement followed by a historic documentary of issues such as, "Delivery delayed on project JB-101820 for 18 days, recent action plans stated it was to ship today. What is status?"

There were project tracking programs that monitored project progress with defined actions. But, her intent was to point out problems, not work through each action plan. As the product managers, this was Bob and Kevin's responsibility.

Anika expected Bob and Kevin to make a presentation about their actions to get the product back on schedule, on budget, and meet the sales target. Bob's presentations were clear and defined into simple, logical components. However, Kevin's presentations were like a boring college lecture while he read stiffly through a spreadsheet. When Kevin neared the end of his recitation, he always discreetly looked for approval from either Anika or Bob.

Ten minutes later, Bob and Kevin casually strolled in to the conference room without apologizing for their lateness. They continued their conversation, never acknowledging anyone else in the room. "Hey Kevin, after this meeting can you show me how you made those pricing models?"

"Sure, and can you show me your product-launch process?"

"Yeah, buddy, no problem."

Huffing, Anika took control of the already late meeting. "Ok, so are you guys ready to make your presentations? Bob, why don't you go first?"

"Sure, good morning everyone. So, last week I showed sales for the new line of commercial products, namely the E1 HVAC system that is not meeting target."

Anika stopped listening after Bob started talking and started to type another grievance letter to Peter. Peter and the VPs do not attend the Monday morning business update meeting. Peter is rarely in his office because he is meeting with clients and establishing new distribution channels. Sam, the VP of Sales, thinks the meeting is Anika's role and expects her to handle these details. Daryl, the VP of Finance, just doesn't want to go to a 9 am meeting.

When Peter is actually in the office, Anika, Sam, and Daryl wrestle each other to see who can muster more time with Peter. Usually though Peter calls one of them to his office for an impromptu update.

Sam grew up just outside of Boston, and went to college in upstate New York. As the VP of sales for more than 10 years, Sam's knowledge of the industry, products, and competitors is extensive. Sam believes this role to be second in command, partially because it includes supervisory responsibilities over both Bob and Kevin. It also requires being a mentor to Anika and Daryl. However, over the past couple of years, things have begun to slip and no one else seems to recognize these perceived "facts."

Daryl bounced from a variety of mid-sized companies and became the Finance VP six years ago after one of his divorces. He is a workaholic and alcoholic...sometimes spending nights in the office hugging a bottle of whiskey. He can recall business numbers without the help of a computer but lacks interest to support Peter in developing business strategies. Daryl is generally not interested in researching new business methods or promoting efficiencies. However, he readily adopts improvements if he can see the benefits.

Bob went to high school and college locally. He is brilliant in business and has a carefree, friendly attitude. He can get along with anyone and can talk all day about almost any topic.

Kevin constantly compares his achievements to Anika and Bob. He immigrated here during college and the office staff nicknamed him "Netflix" because of his frequent references to the latest video trends.

Today's business update meeting lasted until lunch time with Anika, Bob, and Kevin verbally arm wrestling each other about not having enough time to do work. Yet, none of them spoke about the number of meetings they attend throughout the week. In the final minutes of the match, Anika told them both they need to understand staff workloads and to prioritize their projects better.

On the way out of the weekly dogfight, the staff had lingering headaches and were quiet. Feeling frustrated, Nicole, the HR manager, walked out last and asked the staff within earshot if they wanted to go out to lunch for some group therapy.

As they enjoyed their lunch away from office fighting, the staff chatted about not having enough time to get work done. One at a time they chimed in with their frustrations.

It seemed sharing pain was like taking aspirin and hydrating when recovering from a hangover.

Nicole said, "I understand your frustrations. I attend meetings every day of the week with only a couple hours a day to actually get my work done. And sometimes, I have to bring work home and do it on the weekends. I know I shouldn't complain like this with all of you, but I think it is important to get things out there."

Gerald generally keeps a low profile and has been at Pure Air the longest. "I usually can get all my work done on-time, except lately I have missed some deadlines. I get interrupted all the time while at my desk. There is no privacy in the office, and the noise level is getting too high to concentrate." Everyone sadly laughed with him.

Brett said chuckling, "My biggest complaint is that Anika, Bob, and Kevin feed me work every day like I am some sort of hungry dog. They just empty the food into my dish and expect me to quickly devour chunks of it. They seriously expect my work to be completed at the end of the day. I like to be busy but somedays it is overwhelming."

Everyone nodded their heads in agreement, then Gerald said with a grin, "Don't be cruel to dogs."

Brett admitted, "I honestly believe we have three masters. When I am not in any meetings, I find an empty conference room, close the door and sit so no one can see me."

Gerald smirked and laughed. "I told you about this months ago. But, now it is difficult to find an empty office because more meetings are being scheduled and I have to fight Brett for an available conference room."

Brett slyly said, "Now I just schedule a room ahead of time. This way I don't have to waste any time searching for a vacant one."

Looking stunned, Gerald said, "Hey, that's a good idea, I should have thought about that!"

On the way back to the office, Gerald casually mentioned, "Did you know a new guy is starting tomorrow?" Everyone looked a little puzzled. "I think Anika hired another person."

Nicole said, "Hey, I work in HR and I don't know anything about a new hire!"

Gerald shrugged and said, "This has been in the works since around the time Mike started."

"Where is that person going to sit? There aren't any available cubicles," complained Stephanie.

Nicole groaned. "You know there are so many HR things to prepare when we hire a new person and I haven't done anything yet. This means I will have to take my work home again tonight."

Mike, the newcomer, was quiet the whole time. "I think I will be let go because I don't know how to do the work

Kevin assigns me. He hasn't provided me any training, he just gives me task after task and always tells me my work is sloppy, that I don't know how to prioritize, and in general, is just mean to me. I have very little understanding about the products here at Pure Air, but I am learning from Bob's meetings." Mike looked at Stephanie. "I am learning a lot from you too."

Stephanie smiled. "Thanks. So, why am I always the last one to know what happens around here? If I didn't go to lunch with you guys, I wouldn't know anything."

Gerald and Brett shrugged their shoulders. The reality is more like they overheard a conversation between Peter and one of the VPs.

Mike again spoke up, "My biggest frustration is the volume of emails I receive every day. I receive well over 50 emails and get just as many phone calls. How do you guys get through the emails, attend meetings, and actually get work done?"

Gerald said, "You will get it, rookie. You will find a way to quickly filter important and urgent emails and ignore all the others. You will find your way, young Jedi."

Everyone laughed.

"Well, ladies, lunch is over. Too bad Monday ain't over," Brett groaned.

~3~

MEATBALLS AND KICKBACKS

B ack at the office, Stephanie and Mike went directly to
their cubicles, which are in the middle section of the
office, while Gerald and Brett went to the break room to
see if there were any leftovers from an office lunch meeting. Nicole weaved her way through the cubicle maze
and then along toward the back corner where her cubical
sat at the far end of the office near the executive offices.
Everyone else had their game face on as the clock neared
the next hour signaling the start of an afternoon full of
meetings, emails, phone calls, and the opportunity to get
work done.

Kevin finished lunch with a new client and was walking
out of a conference room carrying a tray of catered des-
serts. Bob was at his desk sloppily eating a meatball sandwich checking out the news for the day.

Gerald and Brett saw "Netflix." Both of them eyed him
and immediately started walking toward him. He taunted
them by swaying the tray of dessert chocolates back and
forth hypnotizing them as their heads swayed in unison.
Kevin snickered and Frisbee-tossed the tray onto the
break room counter. "Here you go, boys."

Gerald whooped, "Yeah, baby." Followed by Bret's cheer "touchdown!"

Kevin laughed at them with amazement watching their quick reactions, nearly devouring a petit four just as the tray hit the counter top.

Bob overheard touchdown, looked over his shoulder and just then a meatball popped out of his sandwich, bounced on the desk and rolled across his keyboard leaving a thick trail of red sauce. He yelled, "Damn it! You guys have got to keep the noise down over there."

Gerald, Brett, and Kevin started laughing when they saw Bob stand up with a big splotch of sauce on the front of his white shirt. Embarrassed, he went to the bathroom to clean his shirt. Gerald and Brett went back to their desks laughing.

As Kevin went to his desk, he saw Bob's keyboard covered in meat sauce. Feeling bad, he began cleaning it. By the time Bob came back, Kevin had Bob's keyboard cleaned and had the cost model printed out.

"Thanks. I am always impressed with the way you handle things."

Kevin laughed and said, "I am impressed that you have the confidence to eat a meatball sub in a white shirt."

"Ha ha, you are quite the comedian. Well, that is the last time I eat a meatball sub here," declaring as he dried his shirt with a paper towel.

Kevin pointed, "Here's the cost model we spoke about. I put your data into it and it seems we have a serious problem."

"What do you mean a problem?"

Kevin ran his finger along the paper in concern. "Well, when looking at various supplier costs for your products, it seems the motor supplier is charging more for your motors compared to mine by 4%."

Bob looked at the data report, "What? This is scandalous!"

Kevin looked around and whispered, "Shush...Let's go into a conference room!"

As the conference room door closed, Bob uttered, "I think we need to get Peter involved with this. It looks like there is some fraud going on here. Wait, are you accusing me of receiving a kickback?"

Kevin looked at him, shocked, with his eyes bulging. "No! Not at all. I think someone is getting a kickback and I have my suspicions."

"Well, looking at the numbers, it does look like we are getting ripped off. We definitely need to involve Peter if there is fraud and we need to keep this to ourselves for now. Can you summarize this analysis and show the problem very clearly? Then email Peter and me saying we have a major problem and we need to meet urgently."

"Yeah, I will keep quiet and will do some more analysis."

"As long as you don't involve anyone else, please study. I am glad you have such solid analytical skills."

"Thanks, I think."

Bob and Kevin left the conference room. The office area went from a lunch-time natural rain forest quiet to an office buzz filled with a harmony of medium-sized stock trader voices with occasional laughs that broke up the rhythm. You could tell lunch was over…it was like someone cranked an old engine faster and faster; the engine coughed a few times then the office came to life with a whirl of disturbance.

Anika walked into the office just as Bob and Kevin left the conference room. For a brief second, Anika thought something was terribly wrong based on the expression on both of their faces. But, then she saw a huge wet spot on Bob's shirt and laughed it off.

Mike and Stephanie were going through emails when Mike said, "Today I am not going to read Anika's email because it takes way too much time and I really don't understand much of it."

Stephanie chuckled. "I haven't read her emails in months. But, I do open them and then put them into a folder just in case she checks to see whether I opened it or not."

"You think she checks if someone doesn't open her emails?"

"Definitely. I think she even checks the time they opened it. And, I think she checks people's work over the next day to see if they read her email."

Mike shook his head in disbelief. "Do you think anyone else does that?"

"Only she would do that! She is paranoid and way too demanding." Stephanie grabbed her arm chair, took two deep breaths and closed her eyes for a couple seconds.

Concerned, Mike quietly said, "I am sorry. I didn't mean to get you agitated."

"No, it's not your fault. Let's just get back to work." Stephanie swiveled her chair back to her computer.

Mike thought he angered Stephanie and wanted to cheer her up but didn't know what to say. Instead, he stared into his screen for the rest of the day.

Meanwhile, the rest of the staff were bombarded with a continuous stream of ticker tape-timed emails, customer phone calls, and attendance at various meetings.

After receiving Kevin's email. Peter texted Bob and Kevin to come to his office. Bob replied, "I can be there in 15, I am in a meeting," which was followed by Kevin's response "Ok, I can be available then." Peter confirmed he would see them in 15.

Fifteen or so minutes later, the two product managers walked into Peter's office. "So, what is this major problem? Obviously there isn't a fire because you wouldn't have waited this long."

"Sorry, it is just that we were diving into this product costing model and found a serious issue with motor costs," said Bob. He handed Peter a print out of the summary and analysis.

Kevin said, "I developed this model so I could track individual component costs over time against other factors."

"Nice. Have you developed this with the buyers?"

Kevin looked at Bob then at Peter "Well, honestly I wanted to see if I could do this on my own. I am extracting data sets from a variety of sources and compiling it. I found that the motor costs are 4% higher than other models." He looked at Bob again.

"Go ahead and tell him the way you told me"

Kevin drew in a breath and said, "Well, Peter, I don't want to cause any problems. It seems as though when Carol started working on the new motors, the costs went up 4%."

"So, are you telling me that Carol, our Engineering Manager, has added 4% onto every motor?"

Kevin confidently looked into Peter's eyes. "Yes. I even think she might be receiving a kickback from the supplier. The data clearly shows that when Carol developed the new motor, the costs went up."

Peter threw the papers on top of his keyboard. Looked at both Bob and Kevin with barely hidden anger. "Who have you mentioned this to?"

"No one. We just found out about it today."

"Email me all of this information right away and do not do anything further. I will look into it."

As Bob and Kevin left Peter's office, Anika saw their faces and realized something was definitely wrong. At first, Anika thought Peter called Bob and Kevin in to his office to scold them about the grievance email she wrote earlier. But, their faces didn't look like they were reprimanded. With their jaws dropped and eyebrows raised, it looked as though they were in disbelief. Anika wondered what just happened. She knew she could extract that from Peter later in the week.

Midway through the afternoon, a few people begin leaving the office while everyone else works until the very last minute of the day. The end of the day is similar to the beginning of the day...staff seem to leave all at the same time. The lobby door is unable to fully close as the hoard files out exactly on the hour; Sam is right there with them and heads directly to the gym. Anika, Bob, and Kevin usually stay a little later to finish writing their last email so they feel like they accomplished something before heading out.

—4—

THE NEW GUY

The next morning Anika stood outside her office observing the frenzied rush through the lobby entrance, letting everyone know she was scanning latecomers, for the weak prey. Mike walked in late. Shaking her head in disappointment, Anika jotted down his name and the time he arrived. She tapped her foot on the ground as if ticking off seconds. Phones started ringing as she whispered to herself, "Time to get to work."

Peter casually greeted staff as he strolled through the office. Everyone noticed that Peter escorted a new guy into the breakroom and thought it was quite strange that Peter would personally escort him. Typically, Nicole met and greeted newcomers and then pompously paraded them around the office.

The lobby greeter's voice distinctly came over the intercom telling everyone to meet in the main conference room at 10 a.m. Just a few minutes before 10, staff strolled into the conference room grabbing any available seat farthest from Peter, who was standing along one side of the long conference table while the newcomer stood on the other side. The last few strolling in had to stand along the wall or choose to sit directly next to Peter or the newcomer, which was very awkward. Most stood shoulder to shoulder next to the doorway feeling anxious. Staff were always apprehensive to sit next to Peter because they didn't want to be singled out for any unwanted attention. Peter warmly welcomed everyone, then gave a short upbeat speech about Pure Air's past. He appeared excited as he spoke about the future with new clients, products, and services. Then he paused. He visibly swallowed all the excitement as his face crinkled, and with a stern face, his speech took a harsh turn.

Sounding very frustrated and disappointed, Peter said, "We are losing our competitiveness! We are slower to the market, our profit margins are declining, and we must change our ways!" He slowly and deliberately looked around the room making eye contact with his staff and said, "We should take pride in the number of hard-working, smart people in this room who can achieve anything they put their minds to." This made the staff's spirit begin to perk up. He likened Pure Air as a company that could create something insurmountable like building a rocket ship and sending it off to Mars. On the crescendo, Peter pointed with his open hand to the newcomer and said, "I met Logan at a conference a while back and was very impressed with him. I have invited him here as a hands-on consultant, expecting him to help all of us achieve a higher level of competitiveness. I would like all of you to warmly welcome Logan to our team." Turning to Logan, he smiled and said, "Please introduce yourself to this group of great team members."

Logan looked around the room, smiled, and for a brief moment it seemed as though Logan was standing at the launch pad with the rocket ship pumped full of fuel with clouds of white evaporated gases oozing onto the platform. Logan's voice carried the same level of energy as Peter's and said, "It is a great morning. We are ready for take-off." The staff felt a new spark that ignited and changed their dormant potential energy to an enlightened sense of enthusiasm. Logan described his vast experience with such passion that you could tell he wanted to help them meet Peter's expectations. "I get the most pleasure from helping people achieve incredible goals" he said with gusto.

Peter thanked Logan for his passion and said, "Logan will be roaming around the office, attending your meetings, as well as having one-on-one sessions. Please be sure to invite him to all of your meetings and again, make him feel welcome here. With an authoritative voice, he ended the meeting. "Thanks for making time for this meeting. Now, let's get back to work!" He slowly started to make his way out of the conference room and others followed suit. Soon only Nicole and Logan remained. There were a number of administrative things to take care of such as access codes, confidentiality agreements, etc.

Nicole looked at Logan and said, "I am not sure what else you need to get started because Peter didn't tell me you were joining our group until this morning. Let's go back to my desk and I will introduce you to some of the staff along the way."

Their coffee cups nearly empty, the two stopped at the breakroom for a refill. Logan noticed the break room was clearly well used, more suited for a garage shop than a mid-sized enterprising firm. There was plenty of open space and a large area for tables including a few small tables with bar stools lined along the windows where three people were holding coffee mugs and chatting. After refilling both cups, Nicole said, "I want to introduce you to this group."

Nicole's friendly demeanor allowed her to break apart the three and she immediately began introductions. "Daryl is our Finance VP, Sam is our Sales VP, and Anika is our Customer Service Director. I am so happy to see all three of you here at the same time, this makes my job easier."

Sam said, "I was excited to hear you say you enjoy working out. Maybe you can come to my gym and workout with us."

"That would be great! I don't know any gyms in this city."

"Good, we can go together after work tonight if you are free."

"Absolutely! I need a good workout and am glad we already have some things in common."

Daryl swallowed and awkwardly said, "I served in the Air Force, so we have that in common. Yeah, sure, we could use someone like you here."

Anika followed with, "We knew someone was starting to-day but didn't think it was a consultant. If there is any-thing I can help you with, let me know. Please be sure you stop by my office before the end of the day." She turned and started to walk away.

Sam said, "If you have time now, can you come to my office?"

Daryl stood to leave. "I will catch up with you later, how about we go out to lunch?"

Logan smiled and nodded. "Great, I'll come to your office now Sam and then come find you later Daryl."

Nicole tried to hide her delight that she could shirk off Logan for a while. "I have so many things to get done this morning, I will see you in the afternoon."

Walking out of the break room, Sam introduced Logan to many people along the way. "This is Kelli he works for Daryl, and Stephanie here works in Sales. Brett is an Operation's Supervisor working for Anika and this is Bob, our product manager. Hmm, where the heck is Kevin? Anyway, he is our other product manager."

By the time they reached Sam's office, Logan's head was trying to grasp all the new information. Chuckling he said, "I don't think I will remember one person's name from that whirlwind."

Sam laughed in agreement. "It would be great if every-one wore name badges like we did last year. I still have trouble remembering names, especially the new people. Last year we changed from card badges to smart keys that attach to a key ring and an app on your phone. Oh, did you get one of these yet?"

"Not yet but Nicole has some more onboarding things for me, maybe she will give me one when I see her later."

"How long have you been exercising? I am pretty diligent about my workout. Do you have a regular routine?"

They chatted about fitness as they finished their coffee. Sam looked sincerely at Logan. "Listen I know you have been to many companies and Pure Air is probably similar to a lot of them. We waste so much time in meetings! Our clients constantly complain that we are slow in our response and late with our deliveries. If you can do anything for us, I hope you can improve our productivity soon."

"Sure. Initially, I will sit in on meetings to understand the culture, business processes, current issues, and competencies. Then, hopefully I can offer Peter some recommendations if not just start making some tweaks on my own."

"I hope you make changes soon." The phone rang. Sam said, "Sorry, I need to take this, I will catch up with you later."

Walking out, he saw the other product manager just getting to his desk. Introducing himself, he said, "Hi, I am Logan." Kevin looked a little startled and said, "Nice to meet you. I am Kevin. I am one of the product managers. I am heading to a meeting, would you like to join me?"

"Sure, let's go." On the way, Kevin carried a laptop and was checking texts on his phone. He rarely looked up to see where he was walking. He had the cubicle sea layout memorized. Logan noticed on the way, people chatted on phones, chatted with other staff, and were looking at their screens. As the staff noticed the two walk by, they didn't acknowledge Kevin but they did give a quick smile to Logan.

As they entered a different conference room than earlier, Logan noticed some staff had their laptops open typing emails while others were chit chatting. As soon as Kevin entered, the atmosphere shifted from warm and amiable to a walk-in cooler. His laptop seemed to immediately project an open action item list on the far wall. He first called on Mike asking him for the latest on project JB-101820.

Mike looked up at the project number, then looked at his papers. "Um, well, um, I, um, I think it was supposed to ship already."

"This was supposed to ship 18 days ago! You were supposed to be checking on this. Why can't we ship this? Why don't you know?"

"I have a ton of things I am working on. I will check today."

"If it doesn't ship today. I want to know the reason and action plan as to when it will ship. You can let me know by the end of today. Also, I want you to babysit this project until it ships. Next item, what's the status?"

Kevin's grilling of the group went on for over 45 minutes. He was rifling off questions and actions as if the staff were being executed by a firing squad. After the last item, Kevin stood up and walked out of the room. Everyone else stayed in their chairs. They all took a deep audible breath of relief.

Logan's head was spinning. He asked openly, "I believe this was a product meeting, right? Is this a typical meeting?" The staff looked at each other. One spoke up and said, "No. This is Kevin's meeting. Go to Bob's meeting. His product meetings are completely different." Then all of a sudden, nearly everyone stood and walked out together. Some people stayed in their chairs and looked at the clock. They had five more minutes before the next meeting started. Logan asked those still there, "Where can I find the business process that supports the action item list Kevin was talking about?"

Mike looked confused. "I am not sure if we have that." Stephanie chimed in, "Sure, we have a business process; I will show you how to get into it. Do you have computer access yet?"

"Not yet but I think Nicole is working on it."

"Yeah, she will take care of it. She's great to work with and will help you with everything like that. What's next on your schedule?"

He laughingly replied, "I don't have a schedule."

"Well, if you have time, we can go to Bob's product meeting next so you can see the difference." Mike, Stephanie, and Logan walked out of the conference room together.

Mike told Stephanie, "I will see you at lunch" and walked to his cubicle. Stephanie and Logan passed some of staff who were just in Kevin's meeting. One of them whispered, "I hope you give Kevin a nicer personality."

Stephanie stifled a laugh and said, "Come on guys, let's be nice to Logan on his first day. He doesn't have to see all our dirty laundry on his first day."

Everyone seemed on-time for Bob's meeting with more people in attendance. Bob casually walked in and warmly welcomed everyone. "Hey Logan, I am Bob, we met earlier. I am a product manager here. Glad you can sit in on this meeting; please sit anywhere. Ok, guys, yesterday I sent out an email with some important items, let's go over them and see if we can take action to immediately close the issue."

Logan instinctively saw that everyone seemed eager to give Bob an answer. He could see the staff felt Bob made them feel important and always gave praise even when praise was not fully deserved. Nearing the end of the hour, Bob thanked everyone. "Great job today. I very much appreciate your efforts. Please work on the items we discussed, see you later." This signaled everyone to get up and leave.

Once everyone was gone, Bob said, "How about joining me for the next meeting. Anika just texted me that she wants to meet about some problems we are having with a client because one of our suppliers is late."

They walked into Anika's office together. Anika was on the phone apologizing to a client, then frustratingly hung up and said, "What the heck is going on? How come we didn't get New York's order delivered on-time?"

Bob shamefully lowered his head. "We just talked about that. I will be sure it ships today."

"Well, what are you waiting for, why not work on it now? I will babysit Logan."

Bob left the room without saying anything. Anika waited until Bob closed the door. "I am kind of surprised you are here but I can see why you are needed. Bob is too nice, he wants to be everyone's friend, he knows our business so well, but he needs help to step up his game."

"Yeah, I was just in a meeting with Bob. It seemed like everyone was in high spirits offering their work results like it was an awards ceremony."

"Yeah, that's Bob, giving out little stickers for a job well done like you get in grade school. Hey, listen, we have tons of problems here. I am trying to hold this ship together by pushing people's heads into leaks with the hope that the ship stays afloat and keeps moving along. I get that you know what I am talking about because I saw you attend one of Kevin's meeting. He is a piece of work, a small piece that needs a lot of work."

Logan was a little surprised at her outburst but tucked it away and said, "Listen, I have a few questions for you. What are your biggest issues? And, how do you prioritize work for your staff? How is this communicated? Anika's mind was absorbing the onslaught of questions as Logan continued. How do you measure success, only by KPIs? And, what are the triggers you use to gage whether you are successful or not?" He took a deep breath, clicked his pen and readied himself to write down Anika's reply.

Logan couldn't help but notice that Anika's voice slowly changed from the initial intimidating harshness to a smooth and pleasant voice. Her posture lengthened, she tilted her head slightly, and her eyes smiled openly. "I am not familiar with KPIs, but this is the first time someone asked smart questions. I am really going to enjoy working with you."

Logan looked up from his paper. He certainly couldn't write that down so he patiently waited for her response. "It is my pleasure to make you more successful and I will explain KPI later but," glancing at his vibrating phone, "It's Nicole. Is it okay that we go find her? It seems she needs something from me."

Anika smiled and said, "Do you have time for lunch?"

"Sorry, I already made arrangements with Daryl."

"Fine. We will get lunch tomorrow but I still want to see you at the end of today. Let me show you where Nicole's office is." Both stood and headed to the door. Outside the office, Anika pointed toward Nicole's cubicle, "Her office is right over there. You can't miss her."

Anika conspicuously noted Logan's walking pace was rather quick compared to others in the office then she headed in a different direction.

Nicole saw Logan walking toward her and just as he approached, she said, "I just completed your access codes for the network and building access. Here is the app and key ring for your phone." After the installation was complete, he asked, "Great, thanks, which office is Daryl's?"

Nicole looked over her shoulder, paused and tilted her head in the direction of Daryl's office. Logan turned then said, "Thanks again, see you later."

As he walked into Daryl's office, Daryl asked "How's your morning going? Let's see if Sam can join us and we can go grab some lunch." The two stopped and asked Sam to join them. All three left the office early, well before the usual lunch time. Over lunch, they chatted more about the Pure Air's history, financials, and strategies.

Sam changed the subject and asked Logan about his workout frequency, his workout times, and what he liked and didn't like. They both agreed their fitness group is a cult-like following and any time they meet a fellow Cross Fitter®, they immediately slip into the lingo.

Daryl laughed at them and joined the conversation. "To the rest of us who don't know CrossFit®, it sounds like you are mercenary soldiers on various code-named missions battling for the greatest number of kills."

Everyone laughed as Sam reluctantly said, "Let's get back to the office, I have some urgent calls to make."

Back at the office, Logan walked to one of the conference rooms and stood in the doorway. The meeting seemed to have no apparent leader as conversations were happening at the same time, which didn't seem to bother anyone. People hovered over one person's laptop while another small group was assembled on the other side of the table. Both groups were using acronyms; some people understood them while others look confused. The conversations were more like a foreign language class where some showed complete com-prehension, while others showed frustration or boredom.

Anika found Mike at his desk and told him to follow her. On the way back to her office, Anika saw Logan peering into the conference room. "Hey, once I am done with Mike, you can come see me."

Anika's door closed behind Mike. She immediately pounced, "This is the third time you have been late since you started. There is absolutely no reason for you to be late. It appears you don't want to be here, especially if you can't be on time."

Mike's face started turning red and he looked down at her desk.

"Do you have an excuse for being late?"

"Well, this morning, I had to clean up my apartment because my dog made a mess."

With a wave of her hand, Anika stopped him. "Listen, I don't need to hear about your personal life. You know you have to be here on time. Nicole will be informed that this is your third time being late and you now have a written warning. One more time and you are fired!"

"I am sorry. Yes, I know I have to be here on-time."

Anika growled, "Just to be clear, if you come to work 1 minute late in the next 30 days, you are fired. Understand?"

Mike replied meekly, "Yes, I understand." Harshly, she quipped "Good. Now, get out of my office and get back to work. You have wasted both of our time."

Logan hung outside Anika's office and captured the last words of Anika scolding Mike. Mike walked out, head lowered, face beat red, nearly in tears. He passed by Logan without making eye contact or saying a word. Logan walked in.

Anika was composed and pleasantly said, "Thanks for coming. We've got a lot to do."

━5━

Birth of a Work Moment

Anika was curious to hear Logan's thoughts.

Logan began, "I attended several meetings and met with the staff" and handed her a paper. "I typically hand this out to meeting attendees." The paper had a list of questions. The questions included: Did the meeting start and end on time? Was the meeting very important? Was the meeting's objective accomplished? Do you think the meeting time or number of participants can be reduced? "I try to get the staff to answer questions right after they attend a meeting."

Anika looked over the checklist survey and asked, "What do you think so far about our meetings?

"There is a lot of potential for improving productivity."

She leered at him. "Can you be more specific? Don't worry. I don't get offended easily."

He rifled out, "Most meetings don't have a clear agenda. Less people could attend. Meetings could be shorter, or more collaborative. There was a meeting I observed that was complete chaos. I wouldn't even have called it a working session." Logan looked at his notes. "Also, I noticed action item formats are different, which makes no sense. And, it seems the staff is not using the business process software system for status updates. This seems very strange. Finally, and most importantly, the office work area seems to promote disruptions."

Anika listened patiently. "I can accept some of those things. What else will you be analyzing?"

"Many things. I will focus my attention on how the leaders engage and motivate their staff to achieve goals. I will analyze how the teams set priorities and how they determine what is urgent and important. And, finally I will see how the leaders conduct themselves when goals are not achieved. In other words, do they swiftly re-calculate the direction and speed like your GPS without barking orders or with attitude?"

"Well, the last part happens to me every time I drive my car. And, you are right. My GPS never gives me attitude when I make the wrong turn. By the way, are you going to use this checklist at my meetings?"

Logan eyed her and said, "Yes, I will be passing it out to your attendees as well, making more notes about productivity."

"Well, I am sure you could derive some improvements just by tackling some of these checkpoints."

"Definitely."

"So, after collecting the meeting attendee check sheets, what's next?"

"Analyze the data, meet with staff, and determine an improvement and training plan. For meetings, I teach key actions the meeting organizer can do before, during, and after a meeting. The results are typically astonishing with less people in meetings, more focus on achieving objectives, meeting times are much shorter, and more work is able to get done."

Anika cut him off. "Ah, I am getting it."

Logan leaned forward. "There should be a desire to gain more quality Work Moments throughout the day. And to have those, there must be more available time without having a longer work day. That means, there must be less meetings and disruptions."

"What is a Work Moment?"

"Glad you asked. A Work Moment is an instance or activity that provides an incremental value to the company and satisfies a personal sense of accomplishment."

"Hmmm, I get it and we definitely need more Work Moments. I can certainly see how this will boost our morale too."

"Bingo! That is so important."

"Is this the main part of your consulting?"

Logan smiled, gave a short laugh, and said, "No, not re-ally. There are many management tools, the key is to implement ones that have an immediate impact. Some people will think this is not needed while others will welcome the learning opportunity, and just a small percentage will simply not want to change their ways. Staff will say we have always done it this way and it works fine. But, business environment changes, business practices evolve, and people need to keep updated on both to remain competitive."

"Well, that is certainly true! We need to continuously analyze our business environment, our business practices, and how well we adapt and thrive. I have never thought about it this way."

—6—

ANIKA'S INTERVIEW
AND THOUGHTS

Anika arrived home that night exhausted. As she began to unwind, she relived the day's activities. She went over her discussion with Mike and realized she felt like nothing more than a babysitter, all to make sure people showed up on time!

Smiling, she remembered her talk with Logan and realized she was excited to have outside help and hoped he would be able to suggest some changes. With a snicker, she said to herself, *"That is as long as he doesn't get in my way!"* Suddenly, memories of her own initial interview creeped in as the memory of her sitting with Nicole and Sam for the first time came into focus.

"This is a new role for our company. The customer service staff will report to this new position titled, Director of Customer Service. Currently they report to our Sales VP. We invited you to this interview because we believe you might be a good fit. However, I have a few questions that perhaps you can clarify," said Nicole.

Anika looked at Sam then Nicole and said, "Sure, go ahead."

"Sam, thanks for letting me ask a few questions first. Anika, your resume shows a few different companies each with a short work period of one to three years. You only lasted one year at your last job. Can you explain why you seem to leave after a short time?"

Anika scooted her chair closer to the conference room table. She instinctively knew to look at the decision maker, in this case Sam, but also to occasionally look at Nicole. She confidently responded to Nicole's question. "I left the most recent position after some extenuating circumstances that honestly were unprofessional and I could not work for an unethical company. The business before that offered me a manager level role but the position was more of a senior call center role. The only supervisory experience I had was on the weekends when the manager was not at work. I felt I learned a lot but it was not what I wanted. And, the company prior to that was a supervisory role but I was a supervisor of only three people. So, I left because I wanted a much larger role."

Anika gaged Sam's body language positively and she saw Sam write the word, "Ok" three times next to each of her resume roles." Inwardly she gave herself a pat on the back. She was pretty sure she won over Sam.

Sam thoughtfully looked at the notes on the paper and said, "I want to dig a little deeper into the unethical practice. Can you tell us more about that?"

"It troubles me to talk about that because it was quite personal."

Sam said with dismay, "That's fine. If it is uncomfortable you don't have to elaborate."

Nicole was troubled by the exchange between Sam and Anika. "I get it that you wanted a larger role. Being a supervisor for the weekend is a good step to becoming a manager. Why didn't you want to put in the time and grow in that company? They are a large, recognized firm."

"You are right they are large. To be honest, I didn't think I would get noticed working mainly on the weekends because all of the management worked weekdays. I probably could have worked years in that role and never been noticed. There was no way the current manager would have allowed me to work her shift."

"Well, thank you very much for coming here today," said Sam.

Nicole blinked her eyes several times. She could not believe Sam just ended the interview. "Next stop is to meet our owner and general manager." As Nicole escorted Anika through the cubicle maze, the staff wondered who this new hire was.

After the introductions, Peter said, "Since you made it through Nicole and Sam's interview, I am the final gate." Nicole handed Anika's resume to Peter and he put it on the desk without even glancing at it. "Why do you want to work here?"

Peter could almost see Anika's heart beat through her blouse. She cleared her throat, blinked a couple times, swallowed, and took a deep breath. "From my research, Pure Air seems to be growing against some big competitors. I believe it is not just because of your robust product portfolio but perhaps an enthusiastic customer service support team or a team that works very well together. I have a very competitive personality and I like to win. I am sure I can coach and further develop this team."

Peter looked at Nicole and smiled. "Glad to hear that. What weaknesses do you have?"

"Some people have said I have high standards, am quite disciplined, and can argue as good as any lawyer."

"I wouldn't call any of those weaknesses. We could use more discipline around here. Not so sure about having more lawyers though." He laughed and then said, "Any questions for me?"

"What would be my responsibilities?"

"Nicole can cover all the details with you. There are only two things I am looking for: You will be responsible for ensuring all the customer service team starts work on time and meet the key work performance expectations."

That night, too early to sleep, Anika sat on the bed reminiscing about the interview with Peter over a year ago. Why did I even go to this interview? Am I really unsatisfied? Do I have the confidence to get a higher-paying job with more responsibilities? Peter seems to want to hire me. Every question he asked, I was on top of it. It was almost as if he gave me the questions ahead of time. I think our brain waves were on the same frequency for a moment. He has a nice smile.

But, still, do I really want to leave my job? They gave me an internship, gave me a sign-on bonus, and gave me a hefty salary. I finally could buy a house and car. My parents are proud of me. Ok, except that I don't want to marry Satish. Shaking her head twice, she blinked. How on earth does Mom keep getting into my head? Breath, brush my hair, think of something else.

Pure Air's office space seemed antiquated but the products seemed interesting. Nicole pointed out several of my weaknesses but when I looked at Peter he was writing something. I think Peter already made up his mind about me. Yes, I think he will offer me the supervisor job.

Now what do I do? Oh, no. Was that a mistake? I don't think anyone at work knows I had an interview. Hmmm, I could just go back to work like nothing happened. But, what if Nicole calls HR. That won't look good!

I wonder how much Peter will offer me. The job sounds so much better with more responsibility. If it is 10 percent more I will take it. No, wait. Let's see, it should be at least 20 percent more.

How do people sleep at a time like this? I feel like I am in-between jobs. I like this job all right, but I think this new job can offer me greater potential and more salary.

Shaking her head again, she reminds herself. Look at the ceiling. Nope, that isn't going to work. Getting off the bed, she sighs. Maybe one more session of yoga will ease my mind so I can sleep.

As Anika snaps out of her reflection of times past, she can't help but wish some of Logan's ideas had already been in place before she even started working for Pure Air!

~7~

Another Battle Won

Peter walked to Kevin's desk and scornfully said, "Kevin, when you get a chance come see me."

Kevin cringed, nodded his head, and continued typing.

Bob leaned back and said with a conspired tone, "I know what that's all about."

"Oh yeah, want to tell me?"

Bob scooted his chair closer to Kevin and whispered, "You know, Anika always wants to be number one. She tries to meet with Peter every day and tries to persuade him she is always looking after his best interests."

Kevin looked around to be sure no one could hear him and said, "Don't you think Peter sees through that and knows she just beats people up?"

"I think she tries to manipulate Peter. You and I both know she is pretty good at getting her way. Hey, you better go see Peter. I am sure he is going to tell you to be nicer to Anika and respect her more."

Kevin jumped up. "I already forgot he wanted to see me." As Kevin walked nervously to Peter's office, he glimpsed Anika out of the corner of his eye and felt her gaze. Kevin briefly looked at her and she smirked back as if thinking *"another battle won."*

Peter greeted Kevin as he strolled into his office. "Come sit down. So, I have to ask, why can't you get along with Anika? Is there some cultural issue between you and her? Do you respect her? I just don't get it."

Kevin was shaking and thought, *"Dang, she definitely won this battle."* He swallowed audibly then said, "I think we get along. I don't believe there are any cultural issues." Kevin looked puzzled. "Why? Did she say that?"

"No, she didn't say that. But, she does say that you don't respect her."

Kevin looked at the papers scattered on Peter's desk. "I don't know what to say. I don't treat her any differently than anyone else." Kevin paused and looked at Peter. "And, I don't think I should complain about her."

Peter wanted to delve more into Kevin's complaints, but his phone rang. It was Sarah. "Excuse me, Kevin. We should talk more about this, but I need to take this call."

Kevin got up and walked toward the door and wondered sulkily, *"Maybe I should complain more around here."*

Peter gave a short hand wave shooing Kevin away then answered his phone. "Hey, honey, how are you? Yes, I did. Yes, the appointment is confirmed."

–8–

FREEDOM OF SPEECH, CUBICLE VERSION

Logan left Anika's office hopeful about the prospect of her razor-sharpening Pure Air's competitive edge. He was thinking about spending more time with her, to define a personal development plan for her and propose it to Peter. Logan started walking toward Sam's office as the business day was over.

Sam was anxiously waiting just outside her office looking for Logan. "Are you ready to go?"

"Um, yeah, I guess."

"I guess you already forgot about working out tonight. Hurry up and get your things, see you in the lobby." Logan and Sam headed out of the office with nearly every other staff member. As they were leaving, Logan noticed it was eerily quiet.

On their way to the gym, Logan said, "Did you notice how quiet everyone was as they were leaving the office?"

"Nope, I have to get my mind right for tonight's workout. I need to get focused."

Logan took a mental note; he wanted to study the office politics and test it over the coming days. He was excited to start training on two topics: Top 5 and Daily Routines. After the workout, they both grabbed some dinner where Logan brought up office politics.

Sam explained, "Every company has politics and we do have problems. I think you know that. Our political strife is mainly along departmental lines with a few caveats because of nepotism and friendship. I am doing my best to align Anika with the Pure Air's direction. She sometimes gets it and other times doesn't, unfortunately. I have to constantly work with her on it. Also, Daryl is a dinosaur. I mean, he is a good guy, but set in his ways, kind of slow and very methodical. I am working with Peter to help Daryl grasp the latest business tools."

The next day, Logan was at the office early. He wanted to catch the early birds to see how they prioritized work each day and for the week. He wasn't the first to arrive because office lights were already on. He saw one of the executive's office lights on and a couple people at their desks humming along.

Stephanie didn't notice that Logan was standing on the other side of her monitor. She was in some sort of spreadsheet trance, then abruptly jumped. Logan said, "I am sorry to startle you, good morning."

"I am sorry too, good morning."

"Do you mind if we chat for a few minutes?"

"All right, what's up?"

"What are the critical few things that have to get done today?"

Stephanie exhaled sharply. "I have to get this spreadsheet analysis done before 8 a.m., the due date was yesterday, and I don't like when people call me out in front of a group especially the way Kevin chides people."

"How about we meet later today?"

"Sure, thanks." Stephanie was relieved and switched back into her vegetative trance.

Logan then saw Bob at his desk and walked over. Bob greeted him with a smile, "Good morning. You have a coffee yet?"

"No."

"Good, let's get some and have a chat." At the breakroom, fresh coffee and a platter of breakfast foods were already on the counter.

Logan grabbed a muffin and took a small bite. "What are your main tasks today and this week? How do you prioritize your work? And do you have a Daily Routine?"

Bob didn't seem to mind the questions. He looked at Logan and saw blueberry syrup around the edge of his mouth. Bob nearly cracked up, turned and started to add hazelnut creamer to his coffee. "At the end of the day, I make a list of items that need to be done the next day and then I look at what could be done over the next few days or so. Then I delegate tasks through email with a priority and due date."

Logan finished the muffin with a few more bites then wiped his mouth and hands as they talked more about how Bob communicates his priority list. "I have a Daily Routine, like every morning before 8 a.m., I try to get some emails and simple communications work completed before meetings and other chaos starts."

"Are your Top 5 items clearly defined for you and the staff? Also, do others have a Daily Routine?"

Bob thought about it for a second while he sipped his coffee. "Well, I could be more disciplined with defining weekly Top 5 actions and can see how it would help accomplish more work. I doubt very much anyone here has a Daily Routine. They typically react to issues as they come up. Spend most of their time putting out fires."

Logan thought for a minute. "Ok, switching topics. If your meetings were canceled altogether or were 15 minutes shorter, how would this affect your productivity and Daily Routine?

"Wow; that would be a game changer! Cutting meetings or reducing them by 15 minutes would be huge. And, having documented Daily Routines would significantly help in productivity and quality of work."

"So, for your meetings, who takes the notes and who is the timekeeper?

Bob shrugged, "I take the notes and I suppose I am the timekeeper because it is my meeting."

"How do you know you aren't rambling on a topic and only discussing the pertinent items with the vital few people you invited?"

Bob sipped his coffee. "Good question. I suppose I could make improvements."

As the hour approached, Bob said, "It was nice chatting with you, but I have to run." Bob rushed to his meeting and Logan tried keeping up.

Bob's agenda items were brought up via an email list. He started to walk through each item without saying anything about a meeting objective. It seemed as if Bob was a tour guide strolling down a historic street gleefully pointing out significant interests while the tour group listened intently and dwelled about the significance before moving onto the next item. Most of the tour group seemed to stay together while a couple stragglers felt a need to take some notes before catching up with the next action item. Time ticked away fairly quickly as Bob looked at his watch, then looked at Logan with a slight panic. Bob said, "From now on, we will try to limit these meetings to a maximum of 45 minutes." The staff all looked puzzled and wondered what just happened.

At the end of the meeting, Logan stepped up and asked, "I would appreciate it if everyone could fill out this brief survey and give it to me before leaving the conference room."

After completing the survey, one person laughed as he handed the completed survey to Logan. Another commented, "Hey, I like the survey questions, I hope this changes things around here."

Logan stayed in the conference room because another meeting was about to begin. The next meeting started almost on the hour, and again there was no meeting agenda, nor objectives announced at the beginning. The leader seemed to randomly talk about different topics that were difficult to link in a business process way. Logan noticed that no one took notes. At the end of the meeting, Logan passed around the evaluation survey and received similar responses, such as, "Hope this changes something around here." Another commented, "I liked the survey and good luck." All morning, Logan continued bouncing from meeting to meeting with occasional stops to meet with individuals to ask how they prioritize work and if they have a Daily Routine.

After one of the meetings, Stephanie came up to Logan. Rather forcefully, she said "I have time now, let's go for a chat outside."

Logan looked a bit surprised, but said, "Sure."

"There is a café nearby. We can talk privately there."

During the walk, they chatted about the rainy weather, hobbies, food, and other small talk. After ordering their coffee, Stephanie took a deep breath and said, "There are many issues to deal with at this place! It seems I have several bosses, each has their own priority and each thinks I report to them. I already spoke with Anika about this because I report to her. She told me to listen to the others but prioritize her work first. I like working for Anika, even though she is demanding. She is fair, but she hasn't really defended me with the others giving me work to do. I think the others just want to take advantage of me. Plus, I really feel like I should train Mike. He really is a good guy, but he is new to everything here and no one wants to train him. Geez, I already am telling you way too much. I am probably going to get fired over this."

Logan shook his head, smiled and assured her their conversation would remain confidential. "Have you spoken to Nicole about these conflicts?"

"Not yet, but I am on the verge of a nervous breakdown and I definitely should speak to her if it happens again." Stephanie felt a little relieved that Logan was trying to help and provide support. On the way back to the office, they agreed to meet at the café again next week.

As Logan was walking through the office, Gerald signaled Logan and pointed to an open area near the windows.

"Hey, it seems you have spent time with a bunch of people and I want to join in the fun."

"Great, let's find a conference room."

"I got it covered already. I booked a room."

Logan was surprised and Gerald said, "Old dogs can learn new tricks. Brett told me I could book a room in advance for just myself. I was like whoa, that is brilliant! I am going to reserve time more often, it is like I have a private office. No one will bother me so I can get a lot more work done."

Logan seemed kind of puzzled and thought he was kind of selfish to book a room for just himself. On the way to the conference room Logan asked, "How do you prioritize work and do you have a documented Daily Routine such as Mondays certain tasks are to be done while another day other tasks are to be done?

Gerald laughed, "You mean I get to choose what work is important and urgent? You mean like daily routines and standard work that our factory has? Well actually, I am sure some of the others told you I have been here the longest. I know how to work the system; I know the business, I know the politics and I worked in the factory. I learned to define my priorities, allocate time a long time ago. Let's face it, being disciplined and focused are very important business skills. I probably could post my top action items so others can view the status as well as start to define daily routines and standard work for me and others."

"It sounds like you are quite familiar with Eisenhower's Important/Urgent Principle." Shaking his head, Gerald shrugged and said "Um, no, I don't think so."

Logan continued, "Dwight Eisenhower first stated what is important is seldom urgent and what is urgent is seldom important. Important means the task is aligned to goals. High importance is related to an individual's "Key Performance Indicator" otherwise referred to as KPI. Interrupting him, Daryl blurted, "So that's what KPI stands for! You mentioned it once before but I didn't get it."

Logan smiled and made a mental note "*I promised to explain this to Anika too*" as he continued, "It is management directing the individual to perform the task, or project team goals. Low importance is related to administrative activities that do not affect functional or business goals. Urgent means the task requires immediate action, while low urgency means there is no deadline."

"Yeah, that makes total sense."

Logan drew a simple diagram with statements on the whiteboard. "The priority to work on various tasks are ranked as:

1. Important and Urgent—tasks to do immediately
2. Important and not Urgent—tasks to schedule (after the above)
3. Not Important but Urgent—tasks to delegate (if possible)

4. Not Important and not Urgent – tasks that don't have to be done any time soon.

The thought then becomes why is this task even listed?"

As Gerald snapped of photo of the diagram with his phone, Logan explained "It is obvious that you would spend your time on priority 1 and 2 tasks and that with improved planning, there may be fewer priority 1 tasks."

"I am totally with you. I am going to send this to a couple staff."

"I am curious. Who are you sending this to?"

"Shush, there are politics here. I am OK with sharing this with everyone in the office, but some people will not accept it if it comes from me. Some people just don't like me and the ways I get things done." Gerald put his phone in his pocket.

"Every firm has politics and because you have been here the longest, you probably know the most about it and might even be a part of it."

"Well, there are some of us that appreciate new tools like you just showed and who will immediately adopt them; otherwise, we are considered dinosaurs and become extinct. I think if you passed it to other leaders and talked to them about it, they would teach their team to use it too."

"I get it. Let me ask, are there some people you wouldn't send it to or are there some people that you don't think would use it?"

"Well, just between you and I, Kevin most likely wouldn't use it and I doubt Anika would either."

When Gerald and Logan were walking and talking on their way to the conference room, Mike overhead some of their conversation. He heard Gerald say he prioritizes work in the way that he wants and about the politics in the office. Mike immediately spoke to Stephanie about what he heard.

Stephanie said, "I knew Gerald was up to something, he is in the inner circle. He always seems to know what is happening around here before the rest of us. But, what can we do about it? Do you think we should tell Anika?"

"Honestly, I don't know what to say or to whom. I think it is better for me to be quiet."

"I don't give a shit anymore, I am telling Anika. This is just unprofessional!"

—9—

STABBED IN FRONT OF THE BOSS

B ob and Kevin were first to walk out of Peter's office after the meeting, nearly hand in hand like newlyweds processing down the aisle, so gleeful and with a strut. Bob looked at Kevin, "Let's go out to lunch, I am buying beers."

"Yeah, I like where this is headed. This is great!"

Anika, Sam, and Daryl followed them out looking much less jovial. Anika asked, "Sam, Daryl, can we chat for a moment?" Anika led them into a conference room and closes the door.

As soon as the door closed, Daryl grumbled "I don't know about you guys, but I feel like someone is forcing me to eat cold plain broccoli for dinner."

Sam complained, "It's much worse than that. I think Logan just screwed us over."

Anika demanded, "So, what are we going to do about it? Logan is undermining us."

Daryl responded with resignation, "I don't know. All I know is I have more work to do. He doesn't know accounting and finance but he can tell me what to do."

Anika dismissed Daryl's comments and looked at Sam. "We need to do something!"

Sam offered, "I don't like these new changes. They don't apply across the board."

"Tomorrow, I will meet with Peter. I suggest you both do the same," insisted Anika.

Frustrated, Daryl opened the door and walked out. He knew there was no changing Peter's mind.

As soon as he was down the corridor, Anika whispered to Sam "He is defeated. There is no fight left in him."

"Agreed. I will talk to him when I am ready. I suggest you make a plan and not just complain to Peter."

"Don't worry about me. I've got things under control."

Logan stayed in Peter's office well into the afternoon. They discussed many topics. At one point, Logan cornered Peter. "I have four questions for you. What is the main objective for this business? Second, what are the key strategies? Third, what activities promote innovation? And, finally what makes people want to work as a team to achieve goals?"

Peter mused aloud, "When did we lose our competitiveness? Crap, why can't we be hungry like we were before? Where did our passion go?"

Logan let Peter's thoughts simmer on his rhetorical questions, then stressed, "The improvements we talked about earlier need to take hold and be nurtured every day and week by you and the management team. I suggest you have one-on-one meetings with each leader every week and keep a laser focus on their specific KPIs and their Weekly Top 5. To make this work, I highly recommend you have a discussion with them regarding morale and whether they think there are more Work Moments."

Peter slumped, "Yeah, I am sure I won't be doing this every week. Can you do it?"

Logan looked at him with bewilderment. "Well, why can't your leaders commit and just do it with their staffs?"

Peter scratched his chin. "Good question. Hopefully, they understand the seriousness of our situation and will be more accountable."

Logan understood that Peter was not going to make time to meet with his team in a disciplined way, even though he knew it was necessary. So, he didn't say anything and there was an uncomfortable silence. Finally, Logan said, "I would like to make a recommendation."

Still frustrated, Peter countered, "If it is one more management task, it will break the camel's back."

Logan quickly responded, "No, on the contrary. This recommendation is more suited toward you."

"Ok, I am listening."

"Please don't take this as an offensive comment." Peter's eyes widened.

Logan confidently plunged ahead. "The overall office décor needs an overhaul. The office needs places where staff can openly chat. Also, they need more places where staff can concentrate and not be disrupted. Would you be willing to move to a new office location, renovate the current one, or have more staff work remotely?"

"What's wrong with the décor?"

"It's dated. It's worn. It's not suitable for having sustained Work Moments. There is way too much noise."

Peter was shocked to hear such criticism. "Do you really think the office décor looks aged?"

Logan replied somewhat jokingly, "Really, Peter? Do you honestly think your office is the image you want to give your customers about Pure Air?"

Peter looked down at his scuffed-up, 10-year-old leather shoes. "Ok, so it looks similar to my shoes. My clients have more modern-looking offices." Not surprisingly, the meeting lasted until the end of the day.

The next day, Logan went to see Daryl. When he walked into the office, he saw Daryl's couch had a pillow and rumpled blanket. It seemed Daryl was sleeping in his office. At first Logan didn't see Daryl because he was standing in the corner somewhat behind a wooden closet; he was standing, wearing shorts and a T-shirt.

Looking around, Logan asked with a touch of sarcasm, "Did you get a good night's rest?"

"As long as I am here, it is fine. Going to my house is too much for me." Because Logan did not want to know any of this guy's personal life issues, he didn't ask anything else.

Daryl looked at him and muttered, "You know at first I was kind of upset about yesterday, but then thought about it last night over a bottle. You have been to many companies and I know you are only trying to help us. Your ideas are practical and we should be able to implement them without adding work. In fact, the way you explained it, my team would have more free time because they won't be in as many meetings. So, after a couple scotches and some takeout, I got to thinking that I want you to spend more time with my team so we can have financial closings on-time with reports within 10 days after month end."

Logan, a bit surprised, said, "Would you like to get some breakfast?"

"Sorry, another day. I need to pick up my office, clean up,

and get ready for a meeting. Could you stop by later so we can develop a plan to get the finance team engaged?"

"Sure! My pleasure. I will set it up." Logan left Daryl's office and thought, *"Maybe the others have had an epiphany too."*

Anika anxiously paced back and forth in her usual spot toward the back part of the office looking for people walking in late. Anika pivoted and saw Logan almost next to her. Stunned, she blurted out in a stern, commanding way, "Can you come to my office?" Logan nodded and they both walked to her office.

Anika took a deep breath and in a polite manner said, "Please close the door." Then as soon as the door closed, Anika began her assault, "So, let me get this straight. You make a couple of observations and expect us to immediately stop on a dime and make the changes you throw out there? You think we aren't busy enough here?"

Shocked, Logan staggered, held up his hands, and said, "Wait.... Wait.... Wait."

Anika continued with her fusillade using her fingers pointing in the air, "First, you have no business telling me in front of Peter what I should be doing. Second, you are not my boss. Third, you are just a consultant. Fourth, I think you have manipulated Peter for your benefit and not ours. And, last but certainly not least, I will determine what changes we will make and I will determine when we implement them, not you!"

Logan sputtered as he tried to halt her rampage, "Hey, hold on. Listen. Hey."

Anika continued her admonishment, "When you have an idea, you come to me! If I think it is good, I will coordinate with my team. I don't need you to try and lead my team. I am their leader, not you." Finally, Anika stopped to catch her breath and refuel her anger.

Logan saw his chance and jumped headfirst into the fray and said, "Hey, listen Anika. I met with many different people here and saw many issues that can be corrected. I thought we were on the same page! You and I discussed these ideas before I went to Peter. I just don't do workshops or make training presentations. I actually get my hands in on issues and help implement changes."

Anika was not prepared for any counterattacks. She was the one in charge and she was the one to give out disciplinary actions.

"How dare you? How could you go behind my back and do this?"

Logan was visibly upset and said, "Excuse me? What in the hell are you talking about? Are you telling me you are pissed off that Peter told you to do something, something I remind you that we previously discussed and agreed on?"

"That's not the point. Do you think I wasn't going to do the things we agreed? Do you really feel it necessary to have

Peter tell me so you look important or think you are earning your consulting fee? I thought we had started off on a good foot, now how can I trust you?"

The berating was not affecting Logan the way Anika sought. His defenses were clearly stronger than Anika anticipated. She needed another tactic to win this battle.

"Please leave my office. I am done with you for now." Then she blocked him from leaving, just to show she had some physical power over him.

Logan decisively squeezed passed her and confidently said, "It is obvious we have problems. And, of course we will talk about this again. I will be back later to talk about Peter's four topics."

"Oh, so now it is Peter's four topics?"

Logan bit his lip lightly and didn't say another word because he knew this was not a battle to fight. He whispered so Anika couldn't hear, "Silence is power."

Just as Logan opened the door, Anika asked, "Just exactly what are Peter's four topics?"

"Really? Clearly, you weren't taking notes. Ok, they are Effective Meetings, Weekly Top 5, Daily Routines and Standard Work." And he turned on his heel and left.

Anika hissed, "Prick" as he walked out. He looked at the

staff seated nearby but none of them looked up. Either they didn't hear the berating or they were so used to hearing Anika yell at the staff that they really didn't want to pay attention.

Logan was mentally processing the conflict on his way to the breakroom where he ran into Bob. Bob always seemed to be in a good mood, like he had a dream life. "Do you have a few minutes to talk about Peter's meeting yesterday?"

"Sure. I am so excited for the improvements you suggested and have already asked the staff working on my projects for their Top 5. I have already started making a Daily Routine template the staff can fill out so I know when they are spending time on my projects."

Logan was astonished by the contrast between Bob and Anika. "Is there anything I can help you with?"

"Not at the moment, but I want your feedback when I have completed some Daily Routines and Standard Work docs."

"Sure, it will be my pleasure!"

Bob gazed around the office. "Have you seen Peter?"

Shaking his head, Logan said, "Not yet. I don't think he came into the office yet."

"That's strange because he missed a customer call and he rarely misses them. Anyway, see you later."

~10~

LUNCH TIME SAVINGS

A nika peers into Peter's office and catches him pacing around in his office. "Seems you and I are thinking more alike every day Peter. I want to talk with you about my next proposal that will save over $200,000 a year but there is a lot more upside for sales and profit. It's almost lunch, maybe we can discuss it after that."

"Order lunch and have it delivered. We can eat it here while we go over it," said Peter. "Please ask Logan to join us."

"Why not hear my idea first before we involve anyone else?"

Peter waved her off and distractedly replied, "Just go order and get lunch. I will take a roast beef sub on toasted wheat with everything and a large iced tea. Then we can talk more."

Anika walked out of Peter's office. She saw Bob and Kevin at their desk, both eating lunch. Kevin looked like he was wolfing down some leftovers and Bob was diving into his infamous meatball sub. He looked disgusting with sauce all around his mouth. Anika shook her head, kept walking and thought, *"Just one more month, maybe two."*

As she paid for lunch, she thought, *"This is a tiny investment for a goldmine return."* She sashayed into Peter's office with a white lunch bag in each hand swaying her pleated skirt back and forth, trying to tease Peter. She see-sawed her bare arms several times trying to allure his eyes away from his screen. "Here's lunch."

Confused, Peter looked up, "What? What's that all about? Oh, right, food."

"Just thought to distract you before lunch."

Anika opened both bags and presented the food with napkins and utensils in front of Peter's screen. Then, she picked up Peter's sandwich and said, "Like a bite?"

Peter swiftly grabbed his sandwich, looked it over, and said, "So, what's the $200,000 savings?" He then took a big bite of his warm beef sandwich that dripped au jus on the paper plate and all over his hands.

Anika took her time and waited until Peter looked at her. She then moistened her lips and said, "As you know, I have been responsible for customer service for nearly a year. I am certain I can do my job along with product management. Basically, I hold a weekly product meeting already with my team.

She took a deep breath. It was the moment to leap off the bridge. Her brain screamed, *"Yes! Right place, right time, and best way to deliver my idea."* I would like for you to consider relieving Bob of his responsibility. I am sure I can do his job along with one of my staff." There was an awkward silence filled only with Peter's chewing.

Flabbergasted, Peter swallowed. "What? Bob has been with Pure Air from the start! That seems ridiculous!"

Anika was prepared and moved her chess piece into a secondary attack position. "Offer Bob a consulting or advisor job. He can still come into work or we can ask for his advice if we need it."

"You know Bob has been here forever. He knows the product extremely well and does great with customers."

"I agree he knows the product very well and has trained my team very well too. I honestly think we can promote someone to take over his role along with Kevin."

"You mean offer Bob an advisor role and fire Kevin?"

She stood with her hands on the desk and excitedly pronounced, "Let's put it this way. My team can do everything they do. As a first step, have Bob and Kevin take a one-week vacation." She leaned in closer to have her blouse nearly touch the desktop. His eyes shifted to her chest. She whispered, "You know this could work." Anika stood there, stared at his face, waited for his eyes to shift upwards.

"I am not so sure," Peter said tentatively as he took another big bite of his sandwich.

"You know I am capable. I am merely telling you something you already know. This is a huge savings opportunity. And, it will help with morale because we will promote the junior staff."

"I was thinking about some restructuring moves. But, it is risky." Peter slurped his iced tea several times, and wiped his face and hands with several napkins.

"What is the risk? Bob can provide advisory support once a month for a few months then he can retire. You know Bob could have retired a couple years back. I think he might be waiting for you to ask him because he feels loyal to you and doesn't want to offend you. I am certain with the right package you can prompt him to leave as well as have him provide some remote support to you as needed."

Peter finished his sandwich and downed the rest of his iced tea. He looked straight at her and asked, "Is that your only idea?"

Anika decided to move around his desk and position herself next to his side. She knew she needed to add a little more pressure and convince him. She knew he was close to agreeing. He needed just a little push.

Peter unconsciously pushed back his chair. "You really are trying to tempt me with this idea, aren't you?"

Smiling sweetly, she again wet her lips and said "So, what's your decision?"

Looking away from her he hesitantly murmured, "I need to think about this."

-11-

PROGRESS, NOT PERFECTION

The next day Logan greeted Bob and Kevin with a cheerful "Good morning."

Smiling, Bob said, "Hey, glad you stopped by."

Kevin, wearing earbuds, appeared not to hear the conversation as he stared at his multiple screens.

Logan continued, "Hey, I had an idea on how to improve your meetings. Please consider posting the Six Must-Haves meeting checklist next to your monitor. That way, you can be more prepared and the meetings will go smoother."

Bob looked a little embarrassed, "Yeah...but would you remind of the Six Must-Haves? Sorry, I can't remember off the top of my head."

"Sure. 1-Leader of the meeting. 2-Purpose, intended goal, or expected outcome for the meeting, 3-Agenda, 4-Note taker and time keeper, 5-Identify the vital few attendees with authority to take action or make decisions, 6-Start and stop on time."

"Yeah, it would definitely help if display those. I will make up a few cards and pass them out to my staff too. That way all of us will remember what they are."

Kevin turned his head slightly, pulled out one of the earbuds and said, "Hey, I just made an update to the product costing model problem. It is even clearer now."

Surprised, Logan asked, "What's the issue?"

"Oh, sorry, I thought you were Bob. Hi. Hey, Bob, have you heard back from Peter?"

Shaking his head and staring at Kevin, Bob replied, "Please don't say anything else! No, I haven't heard from him. Are you sure you sent him the file?"

"I am sure I did but let me check. Oh, damn! The file is in my Outbox, it's probably too large to send!"

"Well, send him the new file and be sure it goes through. We are going to meet with him this morning."

"I suppose this is very serious. I better leave you guys to it." Logan walked away wondering what that was all about.

Later that afternoon, Logan remembered Peter asked him to come see him when he had a chance. Having some time now, Logan walked into Peter's office. Nicole was in there and Peter was yelling, "You call her into your office today and fire her!"

Logan realized Steve was on the other end of the tele-conference when he heard him say, "I really can't believe Carol would do that, are you sure?"

Reluctantly, Nicole reported, "Daryl has confirmed the num-bers and Howard our attorney has confirmed the contracts."

Steve said, "Alright. I will terminate her immediately. She will be gone before the end of the day."

Nicole said, "Just let me know when you do that so I can attend by phone."

No one heard Logan walk in as he stood there speechless!

Peter croaked, "I feel like we have been screwed by Carol and our supplier. Now I know why we lost some contracts. Our price was too high!" Suddenly, Peter turned. "Logan, what are you doing here?"

Looking a little awkward for having overheard the conver-sation, he replied, "Oh, sorry, bad timing. You called me before and wanted to meet with me". Peter nodded and turned his attention back to the conference call.

"Thanks Steve, call me after it is done, good bye. Nicole, we need to be sure this doesn't happen again. Howard wants to update the non-competitive and non-disclosure agreements. You will need to get them signed."

"Sure. I will take care of it."

"Thanks. That is all."

Peter walked around his desk and stopped at his cabinet. Without making eye contact with Logan, he said, "Would you like something to drink? Coffee, whiskey?"

"Nothing for me. Sorry to interrupt your phone call."

Peter pours two fingers of Skrewball.® "I usually don't drink this early. But, I am pissed off!" He takes a long slow sip to savor the smell and taste of the peanut butter flavor, then takes a deep breath. "I haven't seen you in a while, what have you been doing?"

"I have studied the process flow from initial customer inquiry through to product delivery analyzing actual inputs and outputs, roles, responsibilities, timing, key performance indicators, and opportunities for improvements."

"And? What have you found?"

"Several issues. I need to meet with some of the executives to discuss them."

"Anything serious?"

"Not as serious as what you are going through right now. How about I update you tomorrow after I meet with your VPs?"

~12~

MENDING FENCES

Logan saw Sam staring outside the office window. He knocked and walked in, catching Sam still recovering from a groggy daydream.

Logan blurted out, "Hey, yesterday's meeting with Peter did not go as planned. The information could have been presented in a more palatable way."

"Oh, you think that, really? I don't know how you were able to become my friend and nearly the next day stab me in the back. Peter thinks I don't know the business. He clearly is upset with me and then he tells me to do some administrative work. Thanks a lot Logan. You screwed me and you know it."

Logan was stunned but responded, "Hey look, I have no ill will against you; I had no idea that Peter was going to say those things. He must have had those opinions far longer than the brief time I met with him. So, please accept that I am not against you. In fact, I came in here to help you. This world could use a lot more female executives!"

"What are you talking about?"

"Listen, my goal is to make you more successful. I suggest at the start of every morning have a 5-10 minute face-to-face meeting with everyone on your team. Give each person just about a minute to respond to these simple questions, such as: What issues occurred yesterday that are carried over today? What are the main activities to accomplish today? What issues do you need help with today or tomorrow?"

Sam said, "I will think about it. But, I am still upset."

"I hope you try this. At first your team may not want to say anything because they will feel uncomfortable. But, over time, they will be able to do this without you even being in the office."

"I said I will consider it. You really like to keep beating a dead horse."

"Fine. I will leave you to it. I have to go see how Anika is implementing the new tools."

"Yeah, go ahead."

"Oh, by the way, yesterday I noticed one of your sales people panicking on a client call. It seemed like they could not resolve an issue. I think if you asked about their issues, that they would open up more and you would be able to help them solve their issues. I believe they would appreciate your support and it only takes a couple minutes every day to find out."

Sam waved goodbye, "See you, have a nice day." Sam went back to looking out her window.

Logan opened his mouth but didn't say anything else. He turned and walked out a little heartbroken and whispered, "I need a different tactic."

Logan walked along the corridor and saw Daryl in his office. He stiffened as soon as Logan walked in.

"Do you have some time?"

Daryl all but snarled. "I suppose it is better to hear this from you rather than from Peter, so I better make time now."

Logan opened his laptop and showed a calendar, "What is your team working on today to ensure the books are closed promptly on time every month?"

Daryl hesitated, "They are doing their normal daily activities."

"Well, specifically what are they doing?"

"Their normal daily work!"

"But, is it aligned to close the books promptly."

"I think so, mostly."

"I suggest you make a list of all the closing activity details and plan them for the month. Each day, you close those items off that are done."

"Theoretically I can see the benefits, but my team has been doing this for years. They know what they are doing."

"Then why aren't the books closed promptly every month?" Logan said with just a touch of sarcasm.

"Hey...Issues come up."

"Really? Issues are to be managed. Anyway, please consider my suggestion and make a visual board showing the activity and status. This works in every business."

"I still am not yet convinced of this idea. But, I do like having a visual daily tracking status board. I will meet with my team and discuss it with them."

"Once you develop this calendarized month end closing process, be sure to review it with the team every Monday morning to ensure the kick off of specific actions can start and finish on-time."

"Anything else?"

"Nope. Not at the moment."

Logan left and said to himself, "I will take that as a win."

Logan continued down the corridor and approached Anika's office. As Logan approached her office, he could see her frantically typing. If there was an Olympic sport for typing, Anika could be a world competitor. Logan made one step into Anika's office when Anika said, "Close the door we need to chat." Anika was looking into Logan's eyes while still sprinting on the keyboard.

Logan was amazed with her multi-tasking and asked, "How are things going?" Anika hit the return button quite firmly and then there was an uncomfortable silence.

Anika said, "I just sent out an email blast about business process delays, poor communication of issues, no escalation of severe issues, and various other problems."

"Well, ok. I came here to discuss effective meetings, weekly Top 5, Daily Routines, and Standard Work.

"I will listen, but only if it is brief."

"Here are the survey results, analysis, and list of potential improvements."

Anika placed the surveys on her desk and fanned them out almost as if they were at a black jack table where the dealer spreads the playing cards out showing all the card faces before inserting the cards into a card deck holder. Anika sampled a couple surveys, nodded her head in an agreeable way, then sampled a few more. He felt it was good that she read the hand written staff notes directly. She then flipped through to find the analysis and summary of improvements. She read them and replied, "This is some pretty good stuff. I am wondering now why we have not done this before. Do you think our egos limit our potential?"

Logan stopped her from continuing with her rhetorical questions, "Which of those recommendations do you think are important and urgent?"

"Well, first things first. I am will re-evaluate the need for certain meetings based on objectives and outcomes. Thank you for conducting the survey and offering your recommendations. What else do you want to discuss?" as she looks at her Gucci gold and diamond watch slightly dangling from her wrist.

Logan asked, "Have you considered a short 5-10 minute daily meeting with your staff to ask about the weekly Top 5 issues they are working on?"

Anika said, "I have to think about having a short daily huddle. I have 15 people that report to me. Some work is done remotely so having a standup meeting every morning may not be effective. But, I might meet with some individually and some in small groups."

"I like your idea of organizing your team into smaller work

groups. How will you execute this because some of your staff work remotely?"

Anika said in a firm tone, "Don't worry about executing things around here, that's my job!"

Feeling the sting of her words, he said, "Samantha said she would ask her team each morning a few questions."

"Oh, she did? What will she be asking?"

"What issues occurred yesterday that are carried over today? What are the main activities to accomplish today? What issues do you need help with today or tomorrow? I think asking these simple questions can help you react to important and urgent issues faster."

"Thanks. Well, I already ask my staff those questions."

"Ok. But honestly I have not heard you say that each day. I suggest you make that a part of your Daily Routine."

Anika said, "I see where this is heading. Naturally I can derive a Daily Routine for myself and team."

"Great. I would love to see that. Oh, there is one more thing I would like to challenge you on."

Huffing, she said, "You want to challenge me now? Like as in arm wrestling?"

"No, I challenge you to not write emails to your staff for 2 weeks."

"Listen, I need to document issues and I do that by writing emails!"

"Why not just talk with them? Think of it this way, you will be meeting with each staff individually throughout the week and or with small teams every day. Why would you need to send an email?"

Anika thought for a moment. Logan continued, "I think your team can accomplish more by not attending so many meetings and with your direct involvement you can clearly understand their issues, re-allocate work, and determine whether there are system or individual competency issues."

"I totally understand what you are saying but I think I manage better by informing all my staff at one time about the issues and the effect on business."

Logan shrugged his shoulders. "Why not just try my challenge for a week and see what happens."

"Fine! I will think about it."

Logan left her office feeling great. He thought, *"Progress is being made. It doesn't have to be perfect."*

Time ticked by so fast that the end of day was near. Logan went to look for Sam.

Samantha grabbed her gym bag and headed toward the exit. On the way, Logan asked, "How was your day?"

"Well, after meeting with you, I thought about your survey a lot and decided to re-schedule my sales meetings. Tomorrow I am going to try a short daily meeting. I think my team will be a little surprised with my daily involvement."

"You are much further down the road for improving things overall than you realize. I think your sales team will have more Work Moments. Plus, they will have more face time with you." His inner voice whispered, *"Yes! I mended a few fences today!"* He looked at Sam and chimed, "Let's go work out."

-13-

SHARING IS A LEARNED BEHAVIOR

The next day, Logan arrived at work and went directly to the breakroom and saw Peter standing there.

"Logan come on over here. I want to introduce you to my wife, Sarah."

Reaching out her hand to shake his, she replied, "Well, it is very nice to meet you. I have heard so much about you."

"I hope some of it was good," Logan laughed.

"Only some." Sarah looked at Peter then at Logan. "I am joking. Peter has told me that you are making many changes including wanting to move the office because the décor is outdated and worn. I probably have told Peter this a hundred times. I support this move one hundred percent!"

"Ah, I see. Maybe I should just work with you on this matter." Logan lifted his arm to take a swig of coffee, but Peter moved suddenly and accidentally hit Logan's arm. Logan's coffee and chocolate frosted muffin spilled all over the carpet."

Peter looked at Sarah and said, "Are you happy now? What a mess!"

Surprised by his outburst, Logan said, "Sorry."

Sarah laughed, "Yes, this is both of your messes. I honestly hope you can't get out those stains."

Logan went to the sink, grabbed paper towels and wetted them. He then went down on his hands and knees to start blotting the coffee stains. The worn carpet didn't absorb much of the coffee so the stain was quite large. It seemed the blotting smeared the chocolate muffin into the carpet.

"Oops, maybe I should have used a dry towel first to pick up the frosting," sniggered Logan.

Peter looked down at Logan, then shook his head looking at Sarah. "I think both of you planned this. Find Nicole, maybe she can help you clean up this mess. Sarah let's go!" Peter said with a hint of anger.

As they started to walk away, Sarah turned her head backwards and said, "It was nice meeting you. Now, it seems like we will be moving after all."

Logan pushed his hands off the floor and in a kneeled position, he laughed. "I think this may be the last coffee to be spilled on this carpet."

Peter pushed one hand in the air toward Logan and bantered, "Hey, it may be your last coffee here."

Sarah grabbed Peter's out stretched hand and held it as they walked. She leaned into him. "Are you always this mean at work? Try to be nicer to Logan. He is merely pointing out the obvious."

After admitting defeat on cleaning the stained floor, Logan went to see Bob and Kevin.

"Hey guys, I have a question for you. Why doesn't anyone in your meetings take notes? I see a few people scribble something, but rarely do I see note taking."

Both looked up a little startled. Bob replied, "Good question. I never really thought about it. I suppose they can remember what they heard."

Kevin was silent.

Undeterred, Logan continued, "I would assume management would train staff on note taking as well as do a scenario training session during orientation. Have you ever heard of the 7Ws and 1H?"

Both men both shook their head and in unison replied, "No."

"When, What happened, Which, Where, Why, Who, What is happening now, and How did this happen? Those are the questions that should be answered in anyone's meeting notes. Plus you can add some photos or videos."

With a little more gusto than intended, Bob snipped "Well, I can tell you right now that we have never trained anyone with these questions. But, our factory does something like this."

Showing more reserve than his colleague, Kevin answered, "That is quite interesting. I normally take notes wherever I go. I never heard it put that way before but it makes sense. I think it would help solve many problems, especially if we can define the problem clearly instead of just jumping from one action to another. I will give that a shot."

Bob perked up and said, "Hmmm, this is similar to the Root Cause Analysis training we have in the factory."

Logan, happy Bob was coming around, asked, "So, why don't the staff here have Root Cause Analysis training?"

Bob scratched his head, "Geez, that's a good question. We probably would solve problems faster if we had this training."

Kevin looked at Bob. "Does our factory still have this training?"

"They used to. We can call Steve and have him explain more of what they do for training. Maybe they can do training for us here or we could join them on their next training class."

Satisfied, Logan made a check mark on his notepad. "I suggest you guys talk to Nicole so she can help too."

"Yeah, definitely! She could really help coordinate the training."

Feeling optimistic, Logan continued, "Hey, I have another question. Have you attended each other's meeting yet?"

"Jeez! You are quite pushy. You just asked me about this yesterday," chuckled Bob.

Kevin pitched in with, "I think we both agreed we would start to participate in each other's meetings."

"I think both of you will learn a lot from each other." Looking at Bob, "There are a couple tools that Kevin uses that you don't use."

Bob's face crinkled, "Oh, really? I am curious about that because he learned this job from me."

Kevin smiled, "Yes...I did learn from you but I added some project management spreadsheets and follow-up ways to ensure I don't lose track of open issues, but yes, Bob was my initial trainer."

Bob smacked Kevin's back and said, "I am really looking forward to seeing this buddy! You know, open issue lists are already available for everyone to see on a shared directory as well as through the business process flow software system."

Grinning, Logan continued, "I am aware of your differences. Bob engages the staff and the staff responds quite positively." Then he looked at Kevin. "Whereas in your meetings, I am sorry to say this but it seems like the staff is standing against wall similar to a firing squad. The staff are scared and are reluctant to say anything unless you call on them. I think they would prefer to not be in your meetings."

"Ouch, that was quite harsh." Kevin took offense and retorted, "Are you saying I am not a good product manager?"

"Kevin, if you mimicked some of Bob's behaviors, you would receive much more information."

"Well...I am not Bob!"

With compassion, Bob soothed, "Kevin, let's work on this together. I am certain I will learn from you and I think you could probably learn from me."

Grateful for Bob's influence, Logan warmly said "Kevin you are clearly a diamond in this business and I am just offering some polishing material to help make you a brighter diamond. You are great at adapting to various situations and I am sure you will conquer this new challenge." Kevin started to feel relieved and nodded his head in agreement.

"Just keep in mind, the most important part of participating in these meetings is a short discussion afterwards to define a better way of doing things whether it is the business process, open action item list, email communications, or leadership skills."

Again on the defense, Kevin asked "What do you mean leadership skills?"

"Have you ever seen the way someone will come up to Bob and offer all sorts of information whereas no one does the same to you? Wouldn't you want that?"

"Well yes! That would be great."

Again Bob soothed his friend's ego, "Kevin you know me; you know I am always here to help you succeed. Logan is pointing out leadership skills that honestly you need to improve. And, hey, this is probably one of the easiest things for you to do. The staff will love it."

"So tell me what they are? I will start to work on this today, especially if you think it is best for me and for Pure Air."

Relieved to have his cooperation, Logan cautiously answered, "When you attend Bob's meetings, do not focus on the content, focus on the context or the way in which he uses phrases, his tone, his pauses, his questioning style, his body language, his patience, and his praises."

"Hell, I can do that! I can simulate his methods. I do have those traits."

"Please try. It will take time to cultivate. The staff will start to recognize and appreciate you are trying. I am very happy both of you can accept personal behavior changes and be able to discuss this. Let's discuss this again next week, ok?"

Bob excitedly affirmed, "Sure. Let's do it! I am looking forward to it."

Energy and ego renewed, Kevin stood with his laptop and phone; "I have a meeting to go to now and will start those changes immediately."

Logan replied, "Good luck, continue on this path and we will have a chat next week."

Kevin nodded in agreement and left. Bob turned to Logan, "I completely understand what you are saying. I am glad you said it directly to him. It is easier for him to hear those things from you instead of me because Kevin and I are equals."

"Yeah, I get that. Besides, having a short discussion about the process and tools you are both using is very beneficial."

"Yeah, we probably could do a better job at sharing."

Bob smiled, "I am looking forward to it. I will catch you later at the party."

Logan stopped to see Stephanie and Mike. He knows that they work well together and that they regularly share information. They had their chairs facing each other.

"Can we have a discussion about sharing information?" Logan asked.

In unison they replied, "Sure."

"How did sharing start between you? And, what are some of the prerequisites for sharing information?"

Stephanie and Mike looked at each other with amusement.

Shrugging, Stephanie said, "It's simple. I think the two of us make a great team even though we work for different product managers. We sit right next to each other and share many interests. I think most importantly, we respect each other's abilities and know each other's weaknesses. Sometimes when one of us returns from a meeting, we might shortly brief the other person."

Mike confirmed, "Stephanie is great to work with, very open, honest, and willing to share her knowledge. If it wasn't for her, I probably would be fired because she really provides me a lot of training. I also think the most important thing about us working together is that we both want each other to succeed."

Stephanie smiled and whispered, "You just made my day."

Logan watched Peter and Sarah walk out of Peter's office. Peter asked Nicole, "Where's John? Let's get this retirement party started."

Music was flowing out of the breakroom and many of the staff were already eating. Peter waved to have John come join them and Nicole turned the music down.

Peter said, "Sarah, John and I started working together over 30 years ago. We shared many successes and had a few failures." Putting his arm around John, he wistfully continued, "Today is a very special day for a guy I have known nearly all my life. John is retiring and while sad, I just want everyone to know John helped make Pure Air the company it is today."

Everyone applauded as John blushed and said, "Thanks, thanks."

Peter quieted the applause, "Now let's talk about some of our past triumphs, losses, and some embarrassing moments."

Suddenly, the office lights dimmed and a video lit up the screen. The discussions simmered as everyone started to focus their attention. The video was sort of like a combination of a high school reunion and family get together. There were photos and a video of John when he first started and worked in the factory. One clip showed him talking about a newly launched product. Everyone cheered because that product had propelled Pure Air to the top.

After the video, lights turned back on, music and discussions started ramping up again, and staff were diving into the remaining catered smorgasbord. The party went on for the rest of the afternoon.

Logan left the party and found Anika in her office. He jokingly asked, "Are you sending an email to your staff?"

Anika responded with a touch of embarrassment combined with indignation, "I am asking them to send me their weekly Top 5. You know I have mixed emotions about this tool. On one hand I like it because I can micromanage but on the other hand it seems more administrative."

"Didn't we agree not to send an email to your staff for a week?"

"Well, this is different."

"Hmmm; please explain."

Defiantly she quipped, "When I sent out an email asking for the staff's weekly Top 5, I received different formats, some were statements, some were in a spreadsheet, and some stated an issue along with a status. So, I figured I would make a standard format and send it out."

Feeling slightly castigated, Logan smirked and said "Ok, that's understandable. Ensuring the staff use a standard format, having an expected due date, and personal follow-up is very effective."

"I am beginning to realize the benefits of Daily Routines and having Standard Work. I can follow-up with individuals and see their priorities or I can shift their priorities."

"The way in which you use these tools determines their effectiveness just like using the right tool in the right way.

You wouldn't want to use a screwdriver when a hammer is needed and vice versa would you?"

Begrudgingly, Anika replied, "I suppose not. I get the point."

"One other thing. Do you understand the difference between asking your staff questions versus telling them what to do?"

She looked perplexed, "I am the boss and I should tell them the priorities."

"That is exactly my point. You are using a hammer when you should be using a screwdriver."

"Huh? I don't understand."

"It is important for every staff to feel they add value in their job. Share your knowledge of the business and then question them on the ways to improve the business or ask them about things that can be done to achieve certain KPIs. You can ask them about what they think is important, etc. Getting them to think and talk about their ideas is critical for the business to become more successful. In other words, guide them to determine their own priorities."

"Ok, I know what you are saying. Basically it is a form of micromanagement but more oriented to my staff's personal development."

Inwardly frustrated, Logan explained, "It really isn't micromanagement at all. It is a part of servant leadership while developing their capabilities. You already possess many positive characteristics." Logan slowly said each point as if he was solving a crossword puzzle. "Listening, empathy, commitment to helping others succeed, and having a vision for the business."

Snorting, Anika retorted, "Are you done kissing my ass? Honestly though, I know you struggled to give me those compliments, but I do appreciate them. Alright, I will give your ideas a try and let you know."

~14~

The Other Side of What?

"Did you see Monday's agenda?" Kevin asked.

Bob slid back his chair and turned, "No, why, what's up?"

"Seems Anika has moved our presentations to the end and now we only have 10 minutes."

"What the —?"

"Maybe she thinks she can do our job?"

Bob laughed, "Maybe she could." To which, Kevin had no answer, his face reddening.

"Dude, why are you worrying? It's bound to happen someday. Your future is so bright. Me, on the other hand, a whole different game. I know one day Peter will walk over to me and that will be that."

Kevin started to panic, "Do you really think she is working to get rid of us?"

"Absolutely. She is a tiger on the hunt. Don't you see her pacing every morning? Don't you see her in Peter's office for long extended times?"

Resigned, Kevin mumbled, "I really don't know what to do."

"Seriously? I say live for the moment and do the best you can every day. Otherwise, you will drive yourself crazy."

Bob laughingly taunted, "Hey, Peter just walked out of his office. Why don't you go talk with him?"

"No way. If he already has that thought, he will fire me before he gets a coffee."

Exasperated, Bob scolded, "Dude, you really are insecure. Are you sweating?"

"No, but I have a ton of student loans. I am not like you. I don't have any money. I need this job."

Dumbfounded, Bob asked "What the hell gave you the idea I am made of money?"

"You are joking, right? You eat out every day. You always buy a gourmet coffee. You always want to go out for beers. You have a nice car. You dress nice."

"Thanks, buddy. But, I am not attracted to you."

Flabbergasted, Kevin stuttered, "What? What are you talking about?"

Bob laughed, "It just seems like you wanted to date me."

"No! No! No! You misunderstood me."

"Hey, I understood you. You need to relax. I was pulling your leg. I just wanted to see how you would react. Trust me, you will be fine."

Disgruntled, Kevin spit out, "That is called deception. And, that is not funny! I am mad at you. And, just to be sure, I am going to start writing my resume and look for another job."

"I don't think that is a good idea. Why do you want to live your life in fear? If you do that, you always will be a slave to an employer. And, haven't you heard the saying, 'the grass isn't always greener on the other side'?"

"Other side of what?"

"The fence, the fence. Oh, never mind. Let's put it this way: if you like what you do and you get terminated, it was never meant to be. If you don't like what you do, why are you doing it?" With a smirk, Bob teased, "Hey, here comes Peter again. He is looking over this way. You want me to wave him down?"

"What? No! Don't do that. I need another job first."

"You are so paranoid!"

Just then, Peter walked over to Bob's cubicle. "Hey, guys,

how are things? It doesn't look like you two are busy." He looked at Bob and then Kevin.

"Not really. I have all my things done for the week and am just heading out," Bob said casually.

Kevin looked at Peter and sputtered, "Um, I am always busy. I am always working."

Peter looked at his watch, laughed then walked away.

"He knows! He knows! He's going to fire us," uttered Kevin.

Bob stood and started packing his briefcase. "Calm down. You have given me a headache. I am out of here."

—15—

CAT FIGHT COUNTDOWN

"Hi Nicole, it's Sarah. Can you patch me through to Peter? I know he is in the office, but he is not picking up."

"Oh, hi Sarah! Sure, how are things with you?"

"I am doing well. By the way, I will be bringing in a veggie plate for Peter next week."

Unable to control her chuckle, Nicole asked "A veggie plate? For Peter?"

Giggling herself, Sarah conspiratorially replied, "Yes. His doctor told him he needs to eat healthier, so now he has to eat more vegetables. He isn't going to like it but I am going to watch his diet if he won't do it himself."

Nicole looked around and then covered the phone mouthpiece with her other hand so others couldn't hear her. "He never told me. You know, I saw him have some chips and donuts already this week. And, someone brought him some cookies."

"Damn...I know right now who brought him those. Can I tell you something private?" Sarah replied edgily.

"Of course! You know I work in HR so I have to keep secrets."

"I don't like Anika at all. She is devious. She is mean. She acts so friendly around others, but I can tell she really is the proverbial snake in the grass!"

Nicole laughed. "I am sorry, I shouldn't laugh at that. Between you and I, she certainly isn't an angel. But, please never tell anyone I said that. I love my job and I like working for Peter!"

Relishing the fact she has a compatriot in her dislike, "Honey, don't worry. I won't say anything" Sarah chortled.

"Hmmm, I am sorry. He is not picking up his phone but I know he is in the office. Maybe he is on a customer call or something. Want me to leave him a message?"

"Yes, please. That would be great and I will see you next week."

That evening, Peter walked into his house as he normally did and leaned in to give Sarah a kiss. To his surprised, Sarah stepped away.

Concerned, he asked, "What's wrong?"

"You tell ME what's wrong! I called you earlier, you didn't pick up, and you didn't call me back."

Sheepishly he replied, "Sorry, I was busy with a client all day."

Angrily, she sniped, "Really? I heard you were with Anika all afternoon."

"Well, sure. She was in my office."

"I can't count the number of times I have told you I don't like her. She is a snake in the grass!" Sarah opened the cupboard and grabbed a glass successfully blocking Peter's view of her.

Standing, frozen in place, he waited until Sarah closed the door. "Honey, I know you have said that! But, she is very smart and she has some good ideas to make more money."

"Would you like some water? Your dinner is already on the table" she sulked.

Peter looked into the other room and saw only one place setting with food. Confused, he asked "Aren't you eating with me?"

Stiffly, Sarah took off her apron and hung it behind a cabinet door. "No. I am too upset to eat right now."

He looked at her, looked at the dinner, and back at Sarah. Pleading, "Honey, please? Just come sit down and we can talk about it."

"Not tonight. Go eat before it gets cold!" She muttered over her shoulder as she walked into the other room.

Shaking his head, he knew well enough not to follow her at this point. Resigned to eating alone, he washed his hands then moped to the dining room table.

–16–

BUSINESS FLAVOR OF THE MONTH

P eter walked into the office seeing Anika standing with several of her team. "Good morning, what's going on here?"

The group turned toward Peter. Anika said, "Every morning we have a short meeting to review the Top 5 issues for the day and determine priorities or the need for additional support."

"Very nice! I can see your team is doing a great job!" Peter looked at each of their faces with a smile. "Carry on." as he walked toward his office and saw Sam doing the same thing. Peter continued walking to his office, perplexed but excited.

Later in the morning, Logan met with Anika, Daryl, and Sam regarding the sales process activities. During the meeting, Logan asked, "Have you analyzed the whole system including manufacturing? Have you analyzed the ways in which customers go through the sale's process such as calling into the call center yourself? Or, have you studied the process as if you are a customer?"

Daryl reverently replied, "I like when you ask these types of questions. It is like walking into a dark room and turning on a light. Everything is much clearer. To consider the whole process and not just optimize a part of the process should definitely be our focus."

Anika added, "I haven't tested my team yet. But, I can see they are making progress."

"Well, I constantly hear feedback from our customers and many times it isn't good. It is not a specific product, person, or situation. We have many issues" replied Sam.

Logan optimistically stated, "I believe all of you have made great headway in transforming Pure Air's culture. Do get discouraged, there is no quick, overnight solution. It takes diligence, time, training, and discipline."

"But, the sooner we improve, the better we will be" Sam avowed.

Nodding his head in agreement, Daryl added, "I definitely think Logan has injected some powerful changes and I can see our culture changing."

Anika chimed in with, "Well, we aren't pushing a rope, it is more like going to the dentist."

Logan laughed lightly, "That's funny. I get it. Every person goes to the dentist to see what is wrong as well as get a cleaning. Trust me. Things are going in the right direction."

Sam got up and walked to the exit, "Is there anything else? This meeting has already taken too long." Everyone else followed suit, leaving Logan alone in the room. He smirked and whispered to himself, "I suppose this meeting is over."

He left the conference room and caught Nicole in the hallway, "Hey, so, what's your take on the things I am doing around here?"

Stunned by the question, she thought for a minute and said, "From what I hear, most people think the changes are positive, but there are a few people who have some serious complaints. They believe the changes are negatively affecting our culture and they don't like it. But, generally they like the weekly Top 5 and the new meeting format. They don't like the Daily Routines and Standardized Work. They feel it is affecting their creativity and they feel they will be replaced by robots."

Baffled by her comments, he asked, "Robots?"

"Yeah, they feel if you can document their job, a robot can replace them."

Rubbing his chin in thought, "I suppose I can understand their concerns. We all know the future is clearly to have more automation. Many companies already are using automation in their call centers and some are using artificial intelligence."

Nicole moved closer to Logan and whispered, "Let's not

chat about this in the hallway. In fact, I don't think we should have this conversation at all."

Realizing she had a good point, he spoke with less volume, "By the way, how are you handling the staff that doesn't want to make changes?"

Nicole started into a lecture with one hand chopping at the air. "Personally, I tell them that Pure Air needs to make improvements to remain competitive. So, they need to make changes too. When the heads of the teams ask me about it, I tell them to handle it with stronger words."

Logan folded his arms inquisitively. "Such as?"

"Gerald told me he is telling his team that if they don't adopt these changes, then they can look elsewhere for a job."

Letting out a low whistle, "Wow; that is pretty strong. Out of curiosity, how are the staff taking that type of response?"

Nicole was still gesturing toward the heavens and then put her other hand on her hip. "Well, put it this way. I have more complaints about him than anyone else—well, except for Anika. However, I have heard some of the newer employees feel management is more engaged and that feel safer stating their opinion in front of everyone. Before, there were email battles, now there are open conversations. It does appear some learning is taking place."

Logan unfolded his arms and nodded his head in a pleasing way, "That's mostly good news. I appreciate your vigilance."

"It's my job. Let's have lunch next week and we can talk more."

Logan stepped back thinking the lecture was over. "Please keep your eyes and ears open. Sure, let's do lunch."

Nicole suggested, "Does that mean you are buying me lunch?"

"Of course, but we also need to talk about changing the organization structure."

"Shush. We can talk about whatever you want. You are buying lunch" she jokingly replied and with a smile said, "See you later."

Just then, Anika walked by and asked Logan, "Are you still planning to meet with me and Sam now?"

"Oh, right. I will be there in a minute. I have to grab a few things."

Anika and Sam waited impatiently in the conference room. Anika took the lead. "Today's objective is to review our Daily Routines and Standardized Work status." Just as she started to speak again, Peter interrupted the meeting, "Logan could you be available for a meeting after this?"

"Sure."

"Great; meet me in my office after you're done here."

Anika and Sam looked at each other as Peter walked out. Logan felt their tension and calmly offered, "Perhaps he just wants a status update or he wants to discuss something else altogether."

Always astute, Anika blasted, "You might as well go now. He will be upset if you don't see him right away."

"Got ya! You guys can still meet though," he retorted as he turned to leave.

With a great deal of spite, Anika turned to Sam. "What are some of your ideas to get rid of that man? He is driving me crazy."

"Driving YOU crazy? I think a lot of people think that. He seems to think he can do anything he wants here."

Anika reigned in her frustration, leaned in and whispered, "Almost every day I meet with Peter and tell him that Logan is not really doing much here and that he is not needed. What have you said to Peter about him?"

Looking astonished, Sam replied, "To be honest, this topic never comes up. We never discuss Logan."

Clearly dejected, she gasped, "Do I have to do everything around here? Next time you meet with him, bring the topic up! I want Logan gone and believe you do too. We have to join forces on this if we want it to happen!"

As Logan entered Peter's office, Peter closed the door and said, "I know there is some saber rattling going on. Some staff are clearly disgruntled with the current situation."

"Yeah, well that is quite common. Many people get a little antsy when change is brought in."

Peter nodded in agreement. With a wry smile, he continued "The common theme I hear is that you are an obstacle. They can do these improvements without you. But honestly, until you came in, not one of them showed the initiative to do just that. In fact, I would like you to press more buttons and increase the heat. For the good of Pure Air, things have to change!"

"To be blunt, I am not here to cause conflict and strife. I am here to improve your long-term business profitability. Do you think some staff think I will be taking over their job?"

Peter laughed out loud. "Yup; that is exactly what they said to me. I have known some of these people for many years and unfortunately, it is those employees who are killing my business. I don't want to directly discipline or terminate them because I have known them for many years. But, I may have to make some uncomfortable changes."

"I have already been thinking about a re-structuring with roles, responsibilities, and KPIs changing. Also, some leaders and staff will need to be terminated."

With some nervousness, Peter asked, "Please keep those ideas between you, me, and at some point, Nicole. Onto another topic, how are the other changes taking effect?"

Logan relaxed further into his chair, "Things are going well. Some improvements are already being implemented. Most people are adapting to the new ways."

Peter leaned back and chuckled. "This morning I saw both Anika and Sam having a standup meeting with their staff. I think standup meetings are great. I just hope they keep it up. Do you think some people won't adopt these changes?"

Logan inadvertently let out a quiet snort. "Some people have worked so long here that they have become part of the furniture. Their look is well worn, aged, comfortable, faded, slightly scratched and stained. They are barely able to function. So, they won't want to change. However, those long-term employees have a tribal set of knowledge we should definitely extract and inject into our system. I propose we develop a straw man for identifying and collecting tribal knowledge. A straw man is a documented outline structure based on some brainstorming activity."

Peter sat up a bit straighter. "I agree. That's a very interesting process; how do we start?"

"First, we define what tribal knowledge information is. From there, we identify ways to extract this knowledge and ways to inject it into our system."

Massaging his temples, Peter let out an exaggerated sigh. "This is going to be a huge challenge."

"Yup it is. I suggest we start writing ideas on Post-it notes® and put them on your wall underneath the plaque that says transforming ideas into profit. I call it Mind Mapping. It is a way to purge random ideas and get them out into the open. Go ahead, say what comes to your mind. I will put them under the appropriate category."

Thinking out loud, Peter began, "Personal notes, reference lists, procedures."

"Great. How about practices, walking the process, and auditing?"

"Definitely. It is apparent you have done this before. How about old presentations?"

"Very good idea!" Logan wrote it down and felt a sense of accomplishment from getting Peter to try the exercise.

"Just from what we just said, it shows we have a lot of work to do." Peter put his head in his hands and rubbed his hands across his 5:00 shadow.

"Don't worry. We can distribute the effort among the

management team. We should discuss remote workers too."

"Yeah, it is definitely going to be a challenge to extract their tribal knowledge. The only time we engage them is during videoconferences." He perked up a bit and said, "That's okay. I will find a way. I always have."

"I suggest we audit them as well as have them review the tribal knowledge data sets to fill in any holes. Being some of your most experienced staff, I honestly believe they would love the opportunity to be included in this project."

Peter turned to answer his ringing phone. "Hello? Hi darling, yes, everything is all set. Yes, I will see you tonight. No, I can't right now. I feel fine. I will do it later. Logan is here. Ok, I will tell him." Sounding more exasperated, he continued. No, he hasn't worked on that. I haven't decided yet. I will, soon. Yes, Logan and you can work on that. We can talk more about it tonight. Ok, I have to go. Bye."

Logan couldn't help picking up on a couple of key concerns. "Hope things are ok. Seems Sarah wants me to work with her for upgrading or finding a new office," and he laughed.

"In some ways I am glad you are here. Why don't you put this all together into a plan and we'll meet again next week. Ok, that's all."

Logan walked out and said to himself, *"I wonder what is going on with him?"*

-17-

STRUCTURE 101

Logan sent out a meeting appointment for a half-day Daily Routine and Standard Work workshop. Almost immediately after hitting the send button, Anika declined the invitation.

Miffed, Logan called Anika to find out why.

Sternly, Anika shot out, "I am too busy. I have more important tasks to work on. Also, you have already discussed this with Sam and I. Trust me, we can handle it."

"I understand all of that. But, you still should attend. Your show of support will go a long way with your team members. Your calendar was empty during that period so I booked your time accordingly."

"Listen, I just told you that I am not going to go." She barked, leaving little room for discussion.

Undeterred, Logan tried a different approach. "Immediate impacts would be noticed in productivity and quality."

"Listen. No matter how much you talk, you won't convince me to go."

Still determined, Logan thought of yet another tactic. "Peter expects all leadership to attend the workshop and there is only going to be one workshop."

"I know what a Daily Routine is and I know what Standard Work is, I don't need a consultant to tell me about these sorts of things!" Then she abruptly hung up.

Logan was in a conference room by himself and said, "That was rude! If she knew these things, then why has she never implemented them?"

On the morning of the workshop, Logan had breakfast meals laid out on tables with hot coffee and other drinks. He noticed two faces he had never seen were sitting at one of the tables. Taking the initiative, he walked over, introduced himself and welcomed them to the workshop. Tim and Shelly introduced themselves as remote office workers and explained they both have been with Pure Air well over 20 years.

"That's great! I am very happy you could come to this training session."

"I usually try to make a trip to the office every few months" Tim responded.

Shelly chuckled a bit and added, "I have not been to the

office in a year and was wondering who this new guy was, making changes."

"Well, I am glad you heard we are making changes and delighted you both could be a part of it."

Tim tipped his head in agreement, "I am very interested to be here, not because of the routine and discipline needed but to understand and use Standard Work. I want to share my ideas about remote work and thought this would be a good platform to discuss it."

"I am thrilled to meet you Logan and I want to be in on all the new practices."

"We both like working remotely and we definitely know it takes discipline to adhere to a Daily Routine" Tim replied.

"And I also have some ideas to share," Shelly volunteered.

"Perfect, I am glad both of you could make it, let me get the presentation and other things going."

Logan was setting up some of the workshop materials and noticed that Daryl and Sam were coming out of Sam's office, heading to the conference room. Logan and Daryl caught each other's eyes. Daryl looked like his hand was caught in a cookie jar, his face turned red, he looked guilty.

Logan thought, *"Something is up with those two, but what?"*

Logan walked around the room greeting people as several others were lazily walking in. The only people who weren't in the room yet were Kevin and Anika. "The workshop will start in 5 minutes." Logan overheard one of the staff say that Anika was not attending. Logan texted Peter, "Just to let you know: Anika is not at the workshop."

A projection of the agenda lit up on a wall showing times, topic, and presenter. Logan welcomed everyone. "Good morning, everyone. We have two objectives for today. The first is to define a Daily Routine for each person. Our second objective is to break into a few groups and each group will define Standard Work for a specific office activity."

Logan finished presenting the agenda when his phone vibrated. It was Peter asking whether Anika was invited to the workshop. Slightly self-conscious, Logan told the attendees, "Please continue with the next item. I have to take this call with Peter."

Keeping the call short, Logan walked back into the room, embarrassed. "I apologize for taking that call. Can I ask everyone to put their phones on vibrate?" Quite a few of the attendees snickered.

Logan proceeded to deliver the workshop according to the agenda. Nearly everyone participated and seemed enthusiastic. When the workshop was over, only Bob stayed for a bit to speak with Logan privately.

"Over the past few weeks since you came here, there has been a culture shift for us to be more productive. It clearly seems you are a natural leader for us and we need these tools for our business. I am very happy that you joined us. Do you know why Anika didn't show? I thought for sure she would because this would help her group out quite a bit."

Not giving away his irritation at her absence, Logan merely said, "I am not sure why she wasn't here. I am happy that several of her staff were here and it seemed like they comprehended the information quite well. In fact, during the break, I asked them how things were going and they said tomorrow they would start the Daily Routine and that they believe within a couple weeks they would have all the kinks out. I asked if they knew what happened to Anika but they didn't know. They did say they were in contact with her and received several texts during the workshop."

"Well, it seems like there is still a major problem between you two. I knew initially that you and she had some problems, but then it seemed those issues were worked out. I wonder what happened."

"I don't know what is going on with her. I texted her to find out why she wasn't attending the workshop but she didn't text me back. I texted Peter letting him know she was not in the workshop."

"Did Peter reply?"

No longer hiding his frustration, Logan continued. "No. I plan on speaking with him tomorrow because this clearly shows her unprofessionalism, lack of courtesy, and poor leadership, especially when she knew her team was attending. Sorry, I don't mean to speak out of turn by saying that but I am upset."

"You should be mad! I can only imagine your level of frustration. Do you want to go out for dinner tonight?"

"Sure. I should be in a better mood by then."

Logan spent the rest of the day finishing a proposal for Peter.

After work, both Bob and Logan headed out together. Walking to the pub just down the street, Logan received a call from Peter. Pulling out his phone, he said, "Give me a few minutes...I need to take this call. See you in 5 minutes." Bob headed into the pub.

Logan stood outside and answered the call. "Hey Logan, sorry, I was busy all day and couldn't call you back."

Sucking in his agitation, "No problem. I wanted to talk to you about a couple things. Will you be available tomorrow morning?"

"Is it urgent?"

"Honestly, the issues are very important, but they can wait until tomorrow morning." He turned to head into the Pub while Peter ended the call, "Ok. See you tomorrow."

The next day, Logan prepared a summary of the workshop. He wanted to share a couple of proposals regarding an organizational structure change and a regular communications plan. As Logan entered the office, he saw Anika standing in her usual observation deck, staring at all incoming staff. She looked at Logan for just a few seconds before snickering and looking away. Logan could tell the office staff seemed to be more energetic and interested in their work than previous days. When Logan reached Peter's office, he politely knocked and waited for him to respond. However, Peter was listening to music with ear buds on and did not hear the knock. Logan waited, knocked again, and slowly opened the door to find Peter typing away at his computer. He did not notice Logan until Logan's voice was louder than the music in his ears.

Peter engrossed in reading Logan's proposal. Peter gave him a smile and a thumbs up in approval. Logan was wondering how much of the email he read and asked, "Do you have any questions?"

"I like everything you sent. Let me finish reading it. Go ahead and get yourself some coffee and then we can discuss. We can discuss your text message from yesterday too."

Logan walked out the door and immediately saw Anika still standing on watch. Anika looked at Logan and started walking toward him. He headed in her direction but turned to go in the break room. Anika was quick and caught up to him.

Anika didn't say hello, but immediately hissed, "Why are you meeting with Peter?"

"It's something we had scheduled." He grabbed a cup, and started pouring coffee.

Anika, getting agitated, retorted, "How come you can't look into my eyes when I am talking with you?"

"Hold on, let me finish pouring my coffee," then took one step closer to her, and looked directly into her eyes in an intimidating manner.

Anika stayed her ground, not threatened by Logan's advance. "When I speak with you, you should give me the courtesy to look at me."

Logan took a breath, exhaled, opened his mouth, paused, then closed it again. He turned, took one step away from her, and calmly said, "I will try to meet with you later, is that OK?"

Extremely flustered, she stuttered, "That's fine, see you later."

Logan walked back into Peter's office sipping coffee. Peter was just finishing an email. "Let's get this started. First thing is, your workshop was a success, well, mostly."

Logan placed his coffee on Peter's desk and sat down. "The feedback I received was great. What do you mean by mostly successful?"

"You said Anika didn't attend the workshop and without her buy-in and support, Daily Routines and Standard Work won't be implemented."

"I think her and I started off on the wrong foot, then I thought we worked out some differences. But next thing I know, she blind-sided me by not attending the workshop yesterday. Earlier she said she was all for having Daily Routines and Standard Work. Maybe she thinks she is too smart to attend these workshops. I am not sure what she thinks but the optics of her not showing are terrible because her staff was there. Personally, I think it is unprofessional, shows poor leadership, and lack of respect."

Peter abruptly stated, "It was her prerogative to attend or not. What matters most is, I want Daily Routines implemented immediately across all functions and for all our staff. I also want to see the staff following Standard Work. Now, let's review your proposals."

Logan started to day dream as he realized his case about Anika was falling on deaf ears. Snapping out of it, he sipped his coffee and responded, "Right, the proposals. The summary of them are: 1. Increase revenue by over 25% with minimal costs. We can start immediately and completely implement within two months. And, 2. Increase profit by 2-8%. This will take longer because we will need to implement an automated call service center, upgrade the website to include automated ordering. Also, I propose we move to a smaller more modern office or even move into the factory. I think before we continue, we should agree on who has access to these materials, how we communicate these materials and when to communicate."

Peter pushed his keyboard aside and grabbed a notepad. "Let's review the materials and then decide confidentiality later."

Realizing he had Peter's undivided attention, Logan continued, "My concern here is that some of your direct reports will see this information and then take actions that may go against or may not support these initiatives. A strong communication plan is just as important as the project itself."

Peter sat tapping his pen on the pad, waiting to write something down. "Don't worry. We will make a communications plan for each aspect of the proposals."

Logan stood and walked to Peter's whiteboard. "I think for the first proposal, we include Anika but we should not discuss the second proposal with her until we define it much clearer."

Peter dropped his pen on the notepad. "Go see if you can bring her here. Let her know we need a couple hours. Once we make this plan I want Sam and Daryl to be brought in to get their understanding and commitment. Meanwhile, I will speak with Daryl separately about the second proposal and maybe the three of us can work on this together."

Logan walked out of Peter's office both delighted and troubled. His main thought, "how do I approach Anika?" was causing him the most angst.

~18~

TRAINING DAY

Sitting next to Pure Air's newest employee, headphones on and waiting for the next incoming customer call, Anika abruptly asked Terry, "I don't want to address you wrong. Is there a particular name or pronoun that you prefer people use when talking about you?"

Terry's forehead had several beads of nervous sweat forming. "Wow, I appreciate you asking. Are you familiar with the forms of Ze? That is the group I prefer.

Anika nodded and gave zim the thumbs up as the blinking computer screen indicated an incoming call to answer.

Terry was frightened and under pressure. Adjusting zir headset, the trainee tentatively answered, "Hello." Then there was a pause.

Anika pointed to the Standard Work document as the customer inquired about buying a shutoff valve for their hot water heater.

Terry was frozen. Ze looked at Anika not knowing what to do next. She impatiently poked at the instructions for answering a call. Nodding, ze started, "I-I-I think we have that prod-prod-uct," looking to Anika for further guidance.

She pointed at Terry's face, then at her own face, closed her eyes, and took a deep breath. Ze understood to breath deep and focus. Meanwhile the customer said, "Hello?" Still no response from Terry. The customer stretched out the word once again, "Hell-low—? Are you there?" Being drawn out of a fog of fear, ze stated, "Yes, I am still here. Sorry."

Anika pointed to the second line of the instructions. Meekly, her trainee continued, "Can you tell me your unit model number, please?" and Anika smiled.

Ze was sweating profusely and could feel the damp spots spreading under zir arms while entering the customer's model number into the computer. Then asked, "You only need a shutoff valve?"

The irritated customer spouted, "I could have gone to the hardware store to buy this, but decided to call you. Now, I think I made the wrong decision."

Anika pointed to the highlighted section at the bottom of the page.

Zirs eyes rolled to the sky and stuttered into the microphone, "I-I-I am sorry. This is, this is my first day here." Typing "shutoff valve" into the computer resulted in a part number and price immediately appearing on the screen. "Ah, here, I found it. It is part number V58C-1."

Sounding relieved, the customer said, "Yes, there is a bar-code tag on it with that number. How much?"

"Ten dollars and 99 cents."

"Wow, I was expecting it to be much more expensive."

Terry exhaled deeply, zirs shoulders relaxing, head bobbing and smiled at Anika. "Can I get your name, address, and credit card number?"

Anika took off her headphones, gave Terry a thumbs up, stood, and walked away. Ze took another deep breath and continued processing the order.

A few minutes later Anika returned and sat down. "I realize it might be a little frightening to speak with a person on the phone. But, if you follow this Standard Work document, you will do fine. Everyone has a little trouble at first. Terry nodded and confirmed, "Ok. I am ready for another call."

Anika again pointed to the document. "Just remember, every call you get, read through this line by line and type the information into the computer. If something goes wrong, don't panic." Flipping the page over, she continued, See? This is a trouble shooting guide that will help you, such as if the model number doesn't come up". She pointed to the line that said, "Model number not found."

"Ok, I got it. I think I can do better on my next call."

Anika looked at her watch and said, "I won't have time to follow you on this next one. Are you sure you can do this alone?"

Although Terry was very nervous about fitting in at Pure Air, ze tried to sound confident and replied, "I think so. I can handle it."

"Good, I will check on you after my meeting and remember to just read the script."

Logan walked into the lobby mid-morning and proceeded to the break room to get his daily coffee. As he returned to the sea of cubicles, he noticed a new person in the training cube.

Walking up, he introduced himself. "Hey, I am Logan, welcome aboard. It looks like you are already hard at work. Let me guess. You just finished your first sale, right?"

"How did you know?"

Trying not to act surprised by the trainee's sweat stains, "It's a lucky guess. Was Anika here training you?"

"Yeah, she was sitting right there. I was so nervous. She watched me handle my first call. Since then, I have had a couple more calls."

Logan smiled and cheerfully added, "Well, it seems like you did well. Have a great day, good luck."

"Thank you, you too."

Still very nervous and unsure of zir capability to do this job well, Logan's praise definitely boosted zirs confidence.

The computer screen lit up with another incoming call. The trainee looked at the Standard Work document and read, "Hello, this is Terry, from Pure Air. How can I help you?"

"I would like to get a quote for a new HVAC system for my house."

"Ok, please hold on for one second. May I have your name, please?" Terry searched the computer and Standard Work document for new HVAC system.

The customer said, "Nicolas."

"Ok. Nicolas. A new HVAC system for your house. That must be nice. Ok. Can you tell me your full name, address, and telephone number in case we get cut off?"

After typing all of the personal information into the system, ze continued following the script, "Can you tell me, is this a new system or replacement?"

"New. I want a new system."

"Yes, of course. Can you tell me the square footage of your house?"

"Square footage?"

"Yes, I will need to know the size of your house to give you an accurate price."

"Ok, I don't have that information. Let me find out and I will call you back. Good bye."

"But, hold on." The phone line went silent. Terry thought, "*So close! I think I've got this.*"

Turning away from the computer screen, Terry saw several people's heads but not their faces and heard many voices taking orders. Ze thought, "*I just need to make it through the first day.*"

The screen lit up again. Getting slightly more comfortable with this first line, ze answered, "Hello, this is Terry from Pure Air how can I help you?"

Music played through the speaker in the background. A muffled half-crackled older voice said, "I have a coupon for 20% off and I would like to find out how much a new furnace will cost."

"Hello, ma'am. Can you repeat that?"

"I have a coupon and I would like to buy a new furnace."

Terry could barely hear the older woman speak. "You would like a new furnace?"

"Yes. I have a coupon."

Anika suddenly appeared, nudged Terry's arm, put on the headphones, and sat down.

"Yes ma'am. I understand you have a coupon and would like a new furnace. Can you tell me your first and last name along with an address and phone number?"

Anika gave zim a thumbs up.

The woman started to say her name. Terry asked, "Can you spell your name slowly? Is that a B like in baker or V as in victor?"

The customer nearly inaudible said, "B, it is a B."

"I am sorry ma'am. I can't understand. Is it a B like in baker or V like in Victor."

Frustrated, the customer barked, "B, B, B, B."

"Ok, I have it as V-E-R-N-I-C-E, is that correct?"

"No. It is Bernice. Bernice. It is B. Bernice."

"Yes ma'am. I have it typed in as that."

"Can I get your address and phone number?"

Several minutes later, ze finished typing the customer information, and took a deep breath. "Can you tell me about your current furnace? Is it gas, oil, or electric?"

Terry asked several other questions and even looked up the customer's old model and had shown it on the screen. Anika was mildly pleased that ze handled this challenging call.

"Do you prefer to replace your existing oil furnace with an oil furnace or would you like an electric or gas one?"

Anika nodded her head and whispered, "Nice going."

The customer's voice was hard to hear, but ze heard "Oil furnace."

"Good, do you know if you have natural gas in your neighborhood?"

"I think so."

"Does your clothes dryer operate on gas or electric?"

"Gas."

"Ok, let's get you some pricing on both an oil and gas model."

Anika took off her headphones, gave Terry another thumbs up, and left.

Completely exhausted after that call. Terry thought, "*Only 1 sale in 3 calls; I am never going to make the daily quota. This is very hard.*" The trainee took off the headphones, stood up, and stretched. Seeing the restroom sign not far from zis cubicle, Terry started walking toward the facilities passing by several customer service people, all having conversations. Terry thought, "*How come my customers can't speak like that with me? It seems like they are having a friendly conversation with a friend. I really am not sure if I can do this job!*"

On the way back to the phones, ze stopped in the breakroom to get a soft drink and a snack. Anika saw zie walk into the break room and walked quickly to set the record straight. She caught zim off guard with her bellow, "This is not your break time! I told you earlier that I would be back and let you know when you have a break time."

"But, but, but, I had to go to the bathroom. And, since I was already up, I thought to grab a drink and some chips."

"Not here. If you need to go to the bathroom, you wait for your break. If you need a snack, you wait for your break. This is the second time I have told you! Got it?"

Embarrassed, Terry scurried back to zir desk, put on the headset and waited for the screen to light up.

Anika walked back to her desk and ran into Logan.

Logan quipped, "So, how is the new person doing?"

Slapping the desk, she growled, "I think we hire any warm body."

"Yeah, I got the same feeling. I met Terry earlier and noticed he was sweating profusely. Not sure this one is going to work out. Don't you have a recruiting firm that pre-screens people?"

"It is obvious we are scraping the bottom of the barrel. We do have a pre-screening, but I am not sure how effective it is. This is just one more item for me to add to my laundry list for cleaning this place up. Oh, and by the way, Terry prefers to use ze as a pronoun."

Feeling empathetic, Logan said, "Oh? I didn't know. Sure, no problem. How did you know or how did you approach that with zim?"

"Logan, it doesn't really matter."

"Ok. Well, can I help with the recruiting agency?"

"No, I got this. I want it done right! Are you attending my meeting this afternoon?

"Yeah, see you this afternoon."

Logan walked away and thought, "*She says she wants it done correctly, like I do things wrong all the time. She has such an ego; what a bitch!*"

Just before lunch, Anika walked by Terry and could hear the phone conversation, so she kept walking. She saw Peter's lights on and went inside without knocking.

"Excuse me? What's going on?" Peter questioned with a puzzled look on his face as he took off his coat.

Anika walked closer to him, looked him over, and said, "How are you feeling today?"

Peter hung his jacket on the coat tree on top of a few ties. "I am feeling fine. What are you up to?"

"I am breaking in a new recruit, but seriously doubt this one will make it through the day. I am thinking of revamping our pre-screening with the recruiting agency."

"Fine, whatever. What else is going on?"

Peter still stood near the coat tree and looked out the window distractedly. Anika moved closer, just enough to smell his after shave.

Peter turned around, quickly looked down to her red heels, and up to her eyes and said, "I am going to call Camilla, the Miami distributor. Do you know her?"

Anika didn't say anything. She knew Peter could smell her perfume but he seemed focused on making that call. She brought one hand up to her long brunette hair and pushed a tuft over her shoulder so more of her scent could float into his nostrils.

Smiling sweetly, she cooed, "I have last week's sales numbers. Would you like to see them?"

Peter took a step to her side, pulled back his tall black leather chair with dark red armrests, looked at her and said, "Not right now. You can leave the report on my desk."

Undeterred in her attempt to tease him, she put her hand on her hip and swayed it, hitting the desk. "Ouch, that is hard."

Trying to ignore her presence, Peter picked up his phone. "I thought you said you were training someone. I have some things to do. We can chat later."

She leaned over his desk seductively and placed the report in front of his telephone. Peter had a few digits dialed but his thoughts were interrupted by the sweet perfume and her proximity. Moving away from the desk, she slowly walked to the door. She turned and smiled as she looked over her shoulder and bewitchingly murmured, "I will be back later to finish what we started."

Peter forgot what he dialed, slammed the handset into the phone, shook his head and redialed Camilla. He didn't acknowledge Anika leaving.

After lunch Logan wanted to see how Terry was doing, so

he stopped at zirs desk to find it empty. He then went to see Anika. "How's Terry working out?"

"Borderline at best! If ze is here tomorrow, I will invest more time training but I honestly don't think this one will come back for another day."

"Well, I don't know if you realize this, but the desk seems empty now."

Anika looked at her watch. "Well, if ze took a longer lunch, I am definitely going to make a better recruiting checklist and revamp our on-boarding process. I can't keep wasting my time with people who aren't service-oriented and can't handle talking on a phone."

At that point, Logan received a text; "I just thought to stop by and tell you about the missing recruit."

"Fine. I am on my way out." Anika waved off Logan. He walked in one direction while Anika walked to Peter's office. On the way, she scanned the office to be sure no one was coming in late from lunch.

Before she got all the way in to his office, Peter snapped, "Just the person I wanted to see! Camilla has told me several complaints about our customer service team. They won't return her phone calls and she gets transferred or the line disconnects. What is going on?"

Feeling the sting of his anger, she defensively answered,

"I told you earlier there are many issues for me to work on. I am working on those issues as well as trying to get people qualified to answer the phone."

Waving her away, he snarled, "Anika, just go handle it!"

She walked up to his desk and looked down at him. Scowling, she put both hands on her hips and fumed, "I am working on handling all the issues around here."

Peter looked up at her, "Well, I guess you better get moving then. By the way, that new recruit you were training, I heard they didn't last the morning."

"How do you know?"

"I saw him walk out the front door. The receptionist told me that he appeared very uncomfortable and frustrated."

Anika still had her hands on her hips. She turned sidewise, looked over her shoulder, and said, "I am frustrated too, but I keep working at it. You don't see me giving up!"

Peter quickly responded, "And, again... Go handle it."

As she walked out of Peter's office, she said with the faint hint of a smile, "I will see you at the end of the day."

~19~

ISLANDS OF TECHNOLOGY

It's early Friday morning. Peter and Logan are working together on Logan's proposals. "Have you been to our factory?" Peter asked.

"Not yet."

Peter looked at his watch, then at Logan. "Let's go. It will take a couple hours to get there. It's time for you to meet the team there. We can be there and back by tonight."

"Uh, ok, I guess. Let me get my jacket, I'll see you outside."

During the drive, Peter gushed about the company he started. Expressing his life as if he was a mixed martial arts middleweight championship fighter, he pronounced, "I spent years becoming the best in the industry. I succeeded in many negotiations and won many new customers. Some wins are well known in the industry. However, today feels like the day after a championship fight. I am sore, tired, hurting in many different places, and don't know how long it will take to bounce back."

Logan looked at the road ahead and listened intently as Peter kept talking. "I spent years working for other people and knew someday I wanted my own business just like a fighter who has to train for years before becoming a professional. When I was in 7th grade, I attended a shop class and fell in love with industrial design and fabrication. In college, I got a business degree and had several part-time jobs working in manufacturing companies. After graduation I became a project manager. As a project manager, I worked on many different projects from concept to installation. I negotiated contracts, developed budgets, forecasts, and dealt with many fascinating people. Then, one day, I decided to start my own business."

"Wow, that's a great background to start a new endeavor" Logan confirmed.

"The first few years had many struggles, but I forced myself to keep trying every day. That early period felt like amateur fights. Major mistakes were made. I hired the wrong people, fired people I should have promoted, lost my cool with some customers and suppliers. Heck, I even cursed out a customer one day for being too persistent. Many of these negotiations were sloppy and hot-headed. Eventually, I matured, married Sarah, and then got a few lucky breaks. Sarah was my lucky charm, rock, and inspiration. I became more serious and strategic. I started to win more contracts than I lost. I give a lot of credit to people like Bob and Steve, the factory manager, who you will meet soon. The team was great! They worked so well with each other. Pure Air was moving up the ranks in the industrial HVAC equipment and parts industry."

Logan looked out the window and distractedly said, "The scenery is amazing. It changes back and forth from rolling grasslands with cows feeding to deep green forests filled with maple and pine trees. It's nice to get out of the city."

Peter took his eyes off the road and glared at Logan. "Are you paying attention to me or the trees?"

Logan pulled his eyes away from the passing landscape and apologized. "Sorry. Please continue."

Peter went back to staring idly at the highway. Letting his agitation go, he continued without skipping a beat, "Now, we are one of the top contenders where performance really matters. Over the last few years we have become stagnant in sales and just recently, profits started declining. Currently, we are heading into another championship arena and we just aren't ready. We lost our competitive team spirit, our systems are incompatible and it seems harder every year to get basic business information to plan and manage. It's frustrating as all hell and exhausting!"

Logan didn't want Peter to catch him staring out the window. So, he admired the vehicle interior. "I can see that."

"Do you know we have several business software programs that aren't hard-wired together? Hell, they don't even work well. Just take a look at people using their own spreadsheets and cheat sheets."

Sympathetically, Logan responded, "Believe it or not, that is pretty common."

Peter shook his head in disappointment. "I have islands of technology. I have an ERP system that is not being used to its fullest capability. I have a payroll system that does not link to the ERP system. I have a million different sales spreadsheets. R&D uses a different system than the ERP system to control drawings. We don't even have a work-flow process for launching products." Peter took a several long, deep breaths.

Logan attempted to lessen the stress and said, "Islands of technology, that sounds like a sci-fi TV show."

Peter angrily shot back, "This is no joke. When Pure Air was smaller, I had more of a hands-on management style. We looked at the upcoming 12 months, month by month. On my wall I wrote down the major product line sales unit volumes and prices. I invited staff into my office and we would spend a few days developing our business plan. It was not formal by any means, but it was a plan we followed. I have not had those types of meetings in years. I need to have another chat with Sam."

Trying to reassure him, Logan provided, "Well, we are already making changes. And, I am sure when we get back there, the team will be making more changes."

"Oh believe me, they will—and soon. Getting back to the history. We argued about product line unit volumes sold each month for days. Our mission was to have year-on-year unit sales volumes increase. After fixing the forecasted sales unit volume, we put pricing information next to those volumes. Typically, we took unit pricing discussions offline because this was dependent on our competition in each region. I met with our sales leaders every month and worked out detailed pricing strategies."

"Great coordination." Logan felt like an awkward cheerleader.

As if not hearing Logan, Peter continued, "Once the sales wall was completed, we discussed Operations. We discussed inventory costs, labor costs, and capital investments. To be honest, I always admired Steve for executing his plans so well."

Logan didn't have a note pad with him and his phone for taking notes was in his pants pocket but it was too difficult for him to get it. "I can see there have been many changes over the years with people and systems. Do you think adding staff without having a robust on-boarding process contributed to this?"

"Possibly."

"It is clear that certain key business activities are not tied together and are not coordinated with the leadership team."

"Do you think my leaders have difficulty working together?"

Logan looked at the road ahead then back to Peter, and thought for a quick second. "It is obvious to the lowest-level employee that there are problems within the management team."

"Oh? So you are tactfully saying I am not engaging my management team?"

"No, that is not what I am saying. Individually you regularly meet with them for their updates and that is very good, but what is greatly missing is the management being accountable as a team. You should expect them to jointly develop strategies, work on projects, and define actions to support the business as a whole. Since your ERP implementation, silos of responsibility emerged and slowly over time the management team became less engaged with each other. It would help tremendously to develop more standardized processes from initial customer inquiry through to product delivery, including project management. I noticed many of the staff only know their specific customer service activities. It might be good if everyone understood things from start to finish."

"Ah, of course. Very insightful! I can see it from your perspective."

"I think we can easily get your management team to get back to developing business planning activities as in the past. There is a planning tool called SIOPP. The acronym is Sales, Inventory, Operations, Planning, and Purchasing. I suggest every week, we look at a rolling 52 calendar week period with a time fence for firm production and supplier planning. This is nearly identical to what you were doing before but we will use your islands of technology on a weekly basis for inputs."

Peter's eyes excitedly bounced between the road and Logan. "I like the idea of getting everyone up to speed on all the processes! My leadership team needs to be more accountable and I like this SIOPP tool too. Having a plan every week is far better than reviewing monthly reports. You said we roll this out through our supply chain?"

Logan felt like he hooked onto a big fish. With more enthusiasm, "Absolutely! We will also include the longest lead-times for supplier parts as well as include the worst performing suppliers in the SIOPP tool."

Peter turned his head away from the road and chuckled, "Seems you have done this before."

Returning the smile, he nodded. "Several times! Once the leaders implement SIOPP, lead times and costs will naturally lower, resulting in potentially greater sales."

Peter's eyes again darted faster between the road and Logan. Peter sputtered, "Yeah right! How would the lead times naturally be lower?"

"Because the team focuses on order management and manufacturing part flow through the supply chain."

Recognition seeped in, "Ah, quicker coordination and reaction to information. I got it."

"Utilizing tools, such as a value stream map, to visually see the supply chain processes, the team will define constraints and improvement opportunities; challenge current norms and go through iterations of improvements. It will significantly improve the order fulfillment process."

"How do you know we should change our production operations without ever being in the factory?"

"If your competitors are achieving lower lead times, you must have a lot of poor practices or are doing a lot of non-value added activities. It's just common sense."

"Fair enough. I want this SIOPP tool launched. Now, what about the islands of technology dilemma?"

"Once we focus on optimizing the whole system, we will determine which island of technology needs improvement. Then, identify wastes such as waiting times or production batches and remove them. If you get the management team to work together on a weekly basis, they will become more agile and react more quickly to any situation."

Realizing Logan wasn't writing anything down, Peter challenged, "Aren't you taking notes about our conversation?"

"Uh, I didn't take any notes. I don't have my phone handy or any paper. The good news is, I have a great memory!"

"You are joking, right? Don't even try to piss me off right now!"

"Relax, we've got this. None of it is new so we can capture everything once we get back to the office."

~20~

THE AWKWARD CONVERSATION

The evening ride back to the city wasn't visually stimulating. Peter sat in the same comfortable position while Logan played with his seat controls to make it more comfortable including the heated seat option.

They traveled in silence for the first few miles. After getting back on the highway, Peter curiously asked, "So now that you have seen all aspects of the business, where are the weakest links?"

Logan needed to test Peter's loyalty to Sam. "It is clear the sales team is not focused and are not accountable. You seem to accept mediocrity from them."

"Damn...That was a hard left jab! You really think so?"

"You have been driving new business relationships, but Sam and her team aren't picking up where you leave off. It seems you are great at creating new customer relationships, but Sam is unable to convert that relationship into a hard sale with continued sales."

"Is it that clear to you? I want to automate our customer service support, increase the number of service technicians, move the sales office, give more responsibility to Bob and Kevin, and make a few other organizational changes. I have three issues: Kevin, Sam, and Anika."

It was too dark in the SUV to see Peter's facial expression. He nodded in agreement. "I like the sales office move a lot," then briefly gloated. "Kevin is very smart. He knows the business well, but definitely Bob knows it better. Bob is a great mentor to Kevin and honestly, Kevin is a mentor to Bob too. I think you have a winning leadership team there."

Peter squinted as an oncoming car passed. "Then, that leaves me with Sam and Anika. I am going to offer Samantha an exit package. I want to thank her, but now Pure Air has outgrown her capability, and for that matter her passion."

Logan comprehended the serious tone and said, "The staff will see this as a new direction and I am sure they will accept this as a positive change. Where does Anika fit because there will be few if any customer service staff left?"

"That is a dilemma, but I have an idea. We don't have to take any rash action with Anika because it will take some time to get the website updated. She will surely see she has no future when Sam leaves and I promote Bob and Kevin to be responsible for sales."

Peter's face was still shrouded in darkness, partially lit from the dashboard. Logan asked, "What about marketing, or what other plan do you have for her? You are really the only one marketing this company."

"What do you mean by other plan?" Peter almost growled.

"Well." Logan coughed, and then cleared his throat. Quietly and with caution he plunged ahead, "I was working late last week and happened to see you and Anika in your office." Unfortunately, Logan couldn't see Peter's reaction but his tone came through loud and clear.

"First, it is none of your business! And second, what you saw was an accident. Anika tripped on the carpet."

Peter clenched the steering wheel with two hands, finally faced Logan, and growled, "This is not a topic for you and me."

Logan shifted in his seat. He really wanted to learn more about this affair because it could affect how things go down the road. But, he knew it was too emotional, not the right time or place. Not wanting the last statement to fester, he blurted out, "I suggest we have a sales workshop at the factory."

Peter shook his head, exhaled, and thought, "*Damn, I was hoping he didn't see that.*" He went back to driving with one hand on the wheel and acknowledged Logan's attempt to rescue the conversation. "What do you mean, a sales workshop?"

"It is where you jointly develop strategies to sell your products. You can have the team define Pure Air's strengths, weaknesses, opportunities, and threats. From that framework, you can then define strategies and actions."

Peter suddenly changed lanes and passed a car. "If we have it at the factory, then the customer service team will feel stressed and will be concerned about their future. I think it will send the wrong message."

Shaken by the sudden jerk of the car, Logan fretfully grabbed the door armrest. "I understand your point, so we change the workshop name to SIOPP workshop."

Peter thought for a second. "Fine. I like that approach. It gives credence to the factory's culture. The customer service staff won't be concerned. I like that Anika, Daryl, Bob, and Kevin go to the factory; they can meet the people making our products, learn about the culture and manufacturing process."

Pulling into the sales office parking lot, Peter said, "See you next week. I do not expect you to be meeting with Sam next week."

Anika had several intermittent thoughts over the weekend: *Peter did not call or text over the past two days. Something was wrong. It was daring, crazy, exciting, and stupid. Who was it that walked by the door? No one works*

*late except for the janitor, Logan, ah, maybe it was Daryl.
I should find out and do something about it. I need to find
out. Should I talk with Peter on Monday about it? Maybe.*

Monday morning arrived with fog and a heavy drizzle.
Logan's shoes squeaked with every step as he walked into
the office. He couldn't help but be embarrassed as nearly
everyone he passed looked up and giggled. Logan lowered
his head and walked to the restroom.

On the way, he saw Anika in the middle of her sentry
duty. He decided to catch her first thing, "Do you have a
moment to talk about the status of your action items?"

"Listen. I don't report to you! But for your information, my
part is completed" she sneered.

"I was thinking we need to meet with Sam and Daryl.
Which day and time is best for you?"

"Not today. What's wrong with your shoes? We could do
tomorrow morning, check my schedule."

Ignoring the comment about his shoes, he confirmed "I
will send out a meeting notice." He continued his trek to
dry his socks and shoes in the bathroom with the hand
air dryer. Once dry, he called Steve to discuss the SIOPP
workshop. They defined the objective, list of participants,
and agenda. Satisfied with the call's outcome, he went
to see if Sam was in her office and noticed the office was
relatively quiet because many staff were still attending

Anika's Monday meeting. Logan scowled and thought, *"Why is this meeting still going on? She should have cancelled this by now."*

Sam was at her desk rummaging through some papers. She looked up and invited Logan inside.

"Hey Sam, I was wondering, what's the status with the sales process improvement activities with Anika?"

Noticing his odd gait, "It's going well. I gave her some input. Did you work out over the weekend? You seem to be walking funny."

"Yeah, I pushed myself pretty hard. Guess it shows."

"How was your trip with Peter to the factory?"

"Enlightening. The ride was quite long so we had quite a bit of time to discuss many things and the factory has recently been through a number of personnel changes as well as a culture change."

"Steve is always trying to get the factory going but there always seems to be a roadblock, catastrophe. He generally has some type of excuse for not having products available. I think if he ever gets the stars aligned, this company would skyrocket."

With a touch of concern, "You think the only reason for sales not to grow is product availability?"

Sam stopped searching for a note. She looked directly at Logan. Her voice an octave higher than usual, she squeaked, "That is the biggest factor. Also, our lead times are longer than the market."

"Aren't price and quality factors too?"

Sam immediately went into defense mode. "They are, but having the product available or at the market lead time is so much more helpful for our regional sales people and customer service team."

Changing the subject, he reported, "By the way, Peter asked me to have a SIOPP workshop at the factory shortly. I will be reviewing the agenda with him on Wednesday. I hope you can make a presentation about sales."

Changing from defense to confusion, Sam asked "What is a SIOPP workshop and what presentation?"

"SIOPP stands for Sales, Inventory, Operations, Planning, and Purchasing. We will be developing a joint planning tool that will integrate the sales team with the factory operations team. This will benefit both groups."

"Huh, interesting. but I don't think that is needed."

Logan justifying his point without divulging his angst with her attitude continued, "Having a SIOPP tool will help with having products available. Anyway, it would be great if you could present our sales strategy including some recent successes."

Sam reverted to looking for a note she wrote the other day. She was getting more frustrated. "Well, I don't know about this SIOPP tool...I have never heard of it. And, I don't think I will have time to make a sales presentation."

"This is something Peter wants to implement."

Sam appeared quite agitated. "No, this is something you told him to implement and you seem to be able to convince him to do things. I will speak to him."

"Fine." Logan shook his head and left her office.

Immediately after leaving Sam, Logan sent out a meeting invitation for the next day with Anika, Sam, and Daryl. Then he met individually with staff to review their Daily Routine and Standard Work.

Tuesday morning Peter called Logan, "Why did you speak with Sam?"

"I was following up with the sales process activity things from the previous week."

Peter leaned into his speaker phone. "Sam called me last night and was pretty upset about your conversation. It seems you told her there was a sales workshop and that you wanted her to give a presentation. She said you were sticking your nose into her business and were going to order her to make a sales presentation. Listen, this makes it easier for me to deal with Sam, but I need you to not speak with her. I am handling this matter. And, didn't I tell you not to meet with Sam on Friday?"

Logan timidly replied, "Well, um, well, I have a meeting with Sam, Anika, and Daryl in a few minutes."

"Did you understand what I said? I don't think you do. I said don't speak with Sam. Am I clear?"

"But I scheduled a meeting with them."

"Damn it! Cancel the meeting."

"Ok, consider it cancelled and I won't speak with Sam."

Meanwhile Sam and Daryl were in the conference room waiting for the meeting to start. Logan sent out an email canceling the meeting because of another urgent project. No one replied.

Anxiously, he walked to the conference room and stood in the doorway. "Daryl, Sam, I am so sorry. I have to cancel this meeting. I apologize. I have an urgent issue to deal with." He walked away before they could ask any questions.

Sam frowned and huffed, "This consultant is a pain in the ass. He thinks he knows more than anyone else. I think he is trying to manipulate us! He purposely scheduled this meeting and then canceled it in our face."

"There is no doubt he thinks he is our boss. I will speak

with him later!" Daryl assured her. They both got up and left. Shortly afterward, Peter called Daryl to his office.

Daryl casually and confidently walked into Peter's office as he has done many times fully expecting the same sort of questions as usual, such as current status for sales this month, backlog, accounts receivable issues, and cash on hand. He knew Peter did not want him to sugarcoat any issues. He just wanted facts and status, especially if it affected Pure Air in an unfavorable way. Once the door was closed, Daryl started to rifle off the status.

Looking frazzled, Peter held up his hand, "Hold off on the business update please. Let's chat for a moment. You know Logan and I went to the factory last week. The trip was very enlightening and it got me thinking about several things we should do to get us back on top. By the way, when was the last time you went to the factory?"

Daryl looked toward the ceiling and paused, "Let me think. I usually try to make it there at least once a month. I was there two weeks ago, on a Wednesday."

"How was the visit?"

"Good. We validated some of the cost savings initiatives."

"I want you to think about moving there."

Daryl grabbed his chin and thought for a couple seconds. "You know my divorce was just finalized. I could sure use a change in my current situation. Let me think about it. I like the idea, but I am not sure about my team."

"We can work out those details later. I am concerned about you. I want your decision by the end of the week."

"No problem. Is there anything else?"

Hesitating for a fraction of a second, Peter relayed, "One more item. I need you to calculate Sam's bonus earned year to date and for the remainder of the year, plus I want a list of all the perks, benefits, and costs we have paid year to date and the remainder for the year plus any contractual obligation related to her."

Caught completely off guard and recognizing Sam was going to be terminated, Daryl sighed and asked, "When do you need this information?"

"Tomorrow or the next day is fine. I don't want anyone else involved so please get the information together yourself. When you get this done, come see me immediately."

"Fine, I will keep this confidential and only my eyes will see the information."

"Thanks and for the business update, you can give that to me after you get the other thing done."

Daryl headed to his office. He leaned back into his office lounge chair, clasped both hands around the back of his head and drifted into his own thoughts. *"I am both happy and sad. On the one hand, a huge weight has been lifted off my shoulders. I can finally see the light at the end of a tunnel and the new work environment will be a blessing. But on the flip side, I feel so sorry for Sam. Honestly though, she has been like the grim reaper lately, killing our sales and business. With Sam gone, maybe there is a chance for a revival. Peter knows what is best. Ah, the countryside."*

Before calling Anika to his office, Peter worried: *"Should I or shouldn't have a talk about what happened between us? It is definitely bothering me; still not sure."* Putting those thoughts on the back burner, he called her into his office.

Anika, carrying her laptop so she could show her status walked toward Peter's office while she stressed over her own thoughts. *"Should I or shouldn't I have a chat? It will be an awkward conversation. Well, no need to make a decision now. Let's see how it goes."* Snapping out of her inner conversation, she opened the door, smiled and cheerfully blurted, "Welcome back home! I heard it was a successful trip."

"It was. They made many improvements, including a culture change. When was the last time you were there?"

Surprised at the question, she shrugged. "I rarely go there because my team is mostly here in the office."

"Right. But you didn't answer my question."

"I'm not sure; maybe two times this year."

"That's not enough!" Switching gears, he continued, Ok, so tell me what you would do to market Pure Air better."

Baffled by the quick change, she thought quickly to tell him what she thought would be appropriate. "Off the top of my head, my first thought is to call each regional sales leader and discuss their current sales situation and their marketing strategy. I would evaluate their website and their process for identifying potential sales opportunities. Also, I would compare their performance against others using metrics, demographics, and economics. I might even audit the larger sales areas and newest distributors to understand their marketing perspectives. At the same time, I would do a marketing comparative analysis against our competitors in each region. All of this would require a lot of hands-on work in the field and not just analyzing spreadsheet numbers."

About halfway through Anika's dissertation, his thoughts drifted back to his internal battle. Deciding to have the dreaded conversation, he cut her off and blurted, "I just have to say something about last week. It was a major shock!"

Reeling from his disjointed conversation stream, she quickly and confidently replied, "I am not going to apologize. It was something that just happened."

"But it was wrong."

"It was, but it was exciting too."

"No, let's just stop talking about this. It was wrong." Peter feebly attempted to get back on safer ground. "Let me hear your thoughts about our marketing strategy."

As Peter's voice became weaker, Anika grasped the reality that she could continue last week's advances, and honestly believed Peter would willingly participate. For now, she decided to go along with his change of topic. "Well, Sam kind of does this already. But, she does not have a big picture plan. She lacks discipline, details, and doesn't hold representatives accountable for sales."

Abruptly, he interjected, "You need to prepare a preliminary budget for doing the things you just said. I am sure you can prepare this by yourself and you can show me a more thorough plan next week. I have a call to make, let's catch up later for your business update."

—21—

FRIDAY NIGHT AND
STILL WORKING

Logan and Daryl spent most of Friday analyzing a proposal to Peter. Stretching out his stiff joints, Daryl said, "Why don't you go home? It's late."

Following his lead, Logan stood up and stretched. Shrugging, he replied, "All I am going to do is stay in my hotel room, do a workout, and maybe go for a walk or run."

"Your choice. If you are sticking around, how about a couple scotches and pizza?"

"You don't have to twist my arm. I like pepperoni and hot chili peppers."

Daryl wrinkled his nose and suggested, "Maybe we better get two pizzas. I like pineapple and pickles on mine."

"That's gross! Sounds like a good plan."

Several scotches and half a pizza later, Logan leaned back in his chair. "That scotch is kicking in, I better go."

"You should finish the rest of your pizza or take it with you. I know I won't eat that." Daryl got up, walked over to his book shelf, opened a drawer and shook out two pain killers. "My doctor prescribed these for my back. He also said I should exercise more, eat better, and cut down on my drinking," then laughed, and coughed.

"You could always join Sam and me after work. We typically work out together several nights a week."

"I bet you do! No thanks, I will pass on that." On the way back to his chair, he gulped down two pills with a swig of scotch. Then he slowly sunk back into his body-molded lounge chair.

Logan shook his head a few times and said, "Whatever. I am just saying it will help and you will feel better too."

Letting out a snort, "I thought you were leaving?"

"Yeah, I need to get up early tomorrow and go for a run. You can join me if you want."

Waving off that invitation, he muttered, "See you Monday."

Logan saluted him with his tipped glass, swallowed a finger of the smooth liquor, grabbed his pizza box, and left for the short walk back to his hotel.

Daryl normally would finish a half bottle of scotch on a Friday night watching a ball game or two. This night was no different. After sitting at his desk all day, then lounging, his back was tight, and he had trouble getting into a comfortable position to sleep. He got up, walked over to his bookshelf, and took some more pain killers.

Over the weekend, Logan sent Daryl several updates of his spreadsheet. Not having heard from him, Logan texted Daryl Sunday evening and asked him if he had a chance to look at the spreadsheet.

Monday morning, the office was bustling early then went silent because of Anika's maniac Monday meetings. Logan walked in close to noon. He chuckled to himself thinking, *"No one seems to care whether I get here on time or am not here at all."* Engrossed in his thoughts, Nicole startled him and griped, "Nice of you to show up. Why are you coming in so late?"

"I was on a call with Peter this morning. I have to use my hotel if I want to have a confidential call. I really can't count on that here."

Feeling admonished, she changed her tone. "Hey, I was just asking. I know you work hard. Hell, you probably worked over the weekend too; am I right?"

"Yeah, Daryl and I worked very late on Friday. Have you seen him today?"

"No, I don't think so." glancing over her cubicle wall to see Daryl's office.

Concerned, Logan queried, "That's strange. His lights are off. Normally, his lights are on. Did he say he was going somewhere today?"

"No, but I know he has problems with back pain. Maybe he went to the doctor this morning."

"No, we had more work to do on the proposal we worked on Friday. He would have left me a message." Shaking his head, he started in the direction of Daryl's office, "We need to check his office."

Without hesitation, they opened the door. The smell overwhelmed their senses. Both stood stock still when they noticed Daryl lying face up, mouth open, and the bottle of pain pills open next to him.

"Oh my god!" cried Nicole.

~22~

Uncomfortable Talk

Nicole unpacked the work she took home last night and readied her office for another busy day when she noticed a magazine addressed to Daryl on her desk. She thought, *"That's weird. I better drop if off before my day gets out of control."*

Tentatively knocking on the door casing, she quietly said, "Good morning. How are you feeling today? You scared us yesterday! Are you okay? I came to let you know someone left your magazine on my desk?"

"Sorry about yesterday but I am feeling much better. I guess I forgot to set my alarm. My back was killing me this past weekend." Waving her in to his office, "Would you mind closing the door? I have something to tell you."

Nicole anxiously closed the door and waited for Daryl to speak.

"I don't know how to say this, but I think I should mention it before it gets out of control."

Still perplexed, she sat down and looked around Daryl's office. With a nervous smile she joked, "Are you going to say something about you living in your office?"

"What? Oh, No. Well sort of."

Trying to comfort him, she leaned forward and whispered, "Don't worry. I understand your circumstances. And, we all know it is temporary."

Daryl put up his hand to stop her. "No, it's not that. I have something else to say. This is so difficult for me to tell you. But, I feel it is the right thing to do."

Giving him her complete attention, she nodded, "Go ahead, I'm listening."

Closing his eyes and exhaling, he plunged on, "In the past couple of weeks, I have noticed Anika and Peter meeting much more frequently behind closed doors."

"That's not so unusual." She was really baffled now.

"Right, except one night, they were together and they weren't working. Do you know what I am saying?"

"No. I don't. Please explain."

"I don't know what you would call it. It seems like Anika made several sexual advances toward Peter."

She incredulously stuttered, "What? Really? How do you know this?"

"The first time, I overheard Anika talk with Peter after work. She really came onto Peter and it was more than just flirting. On one occasion, I saw Anika step right in front of Peter so her face was next to his, she grabbed both of his arms and put them around her waist."

"Really! What did he do?"

"Peter grabbed her arms and stepped away from her. He said, 'Not here.' Then he walked away. I could tell Anika was mad because she stomped one foot on the floor. I was standing just on the other side of that big plant by the break room." Daryl, now pacing, gestures through his office window in the direction of the plant in question, "I saw and heard everything!" Sitting back down with a heavy sigh.

"So let me get this straight. Anika is flirting with Peter. And, you think Peter is ok with that?"

Daryl stood up again, walked toward his window, and looked out. "I really don't know what to say. But, I know Anika is leading it."

Outraged, she blurted, "And Peter was accepting it?"

Daryl slammed both hands onto the window frame. Then, he turned facing Nicole. "Damn it, one time they were having outright sex. There I said it!" He felt much lighter now that he had told someone.

Nicole's mouth opened wide. She gasped. "Oh, I see. Oh, this is serious!"

Daryl walked away from the window, leaned in closer to Nicole and put both hands on his desk to hold him upright. "And, you know who else knows?"

Responding in full alarm mode, "No, who?"

"Logan!" Daryl collapsed back into his chair.

"How on Earth would Logan know that?"

"On that night, I was relaxing with my lights off. That is when I heard Anika make some advances on Peter in the hallway just outside my door. Then, a few minutes later I heard her moaning. Not even 3 minutes later, I saw Logan walk past my office. There is no way he could have missed hearing and seeing them. He walked right past Peter's office, probably on the way to the bathroom."

"Oh, my. Oh, my!" Nicole sat there shaking her head in complete disbelief.

Daryl stood up and put his hands in his pockets. Sheepishly, he looked at her. "I put that magazine on your desk. I knew you would personally drop it off. I know it sounds crazy and I am sure you didn't expect to hear that this morning. I just don't know what else to do."

Composing herself, she sat straight up and commanded, "You keep this to yourself! I need to handle this carefully. It is going to take me a couple of days to look into this further. I also think I will call Pure Air's attorney to make sure this is handled properly. However, if by chance, Peter says something to you, you better set him straight. And, don't speak with Anika about this or even with Logan. You got it?"

Just then, they both overheard Anika outside Daryl's office, yelling at someone about being late again.

Turning back to him, she lowered her voice, "And, if you speak with Peter, let him know that all this yelling needs to stop. The staff thinks they are in a prison." Daryl slowly pulling out his chair, nodded in agreement, sat down, took a deep breath, then started typing as Nicole got up and left his office.

Still reeling, Nicole was thinking on her way back to her office, *"This morning I made a Top 5 plan. Logan would have been proud. Now, I can throw that away. I need to figure out how to manage this crisis. I need to have a discussion with Logan and understand what he knows."*

Nicole reached her office and sat down. She could still hear Anika yelling at someone in her office. She shook her head and thought, *"These people have no idea about the chaos going on around them."*

Logan had a cup of coffee in his hand and roamed around the office looking at people's screens and observing fewer people texting. He also noticed several people posted their Weekly Top 5 next to their screens. Logan smiled, basking in a sense of accomplishment.

Nicole spied Logan as he walked around the corner and started to flag him down. He was so engrossed in his review of the staff, he didn't notice Nicole waving at him. Frustrated, Nicole lifted her arm higher and continued her attempt to grab his attention. Finally, she yelled, "Logan!"

Logan turned his attention to her and mouthed, "Good morning." She waved for him to follow her as she headed toward an empty conference room. Bewildered, Logan followed her in and watched her turn on the lights and close the door. "Please sit down Logan."

"What's up?"

Without hesitation, she forged ahead, "I have an issue to discuss with you."

Still confused, he asked, "Ok, what's going on?"

Nicole stood in front him. "Just recently you worked late one night, right?"

Logan stretched out the word, "Ye-ah? I sometimes work late here. Is that a problem?"

"Yes, well, no. On one of those nights did you happen to see Anika in Peter's office?"

Logan's face reddened. He thought for a moment, *"What should I say? Did Anika say something? Was it Peter? No, maybe the janitor?"* Nicole waited patiently for Logan to respond.

"This is quite uncomfortable to talk about. I am not sure what to say, how to say it, or what to do."

She sat down across from him and assured, "Please, just tell me what happened." She flipped over her notepad to get a clean sheet of paper to write on, and waited to pen Logan's revelation.

Logan stared at her blank paper. "Honestly, I really don't know what to make of it."

"Just tell me what you saw!"

Resigned, he started, "Ok. Last week, I was working late and I heard something odd. I didn't know what to make of it but it disturbed me to the point that I decided to check it out. So, I got up and on the way to the bathroom, I uh-." Logan shifted in the chair.

"Please continue," Nicole urged.

"I walked along the executive hallway. The lights were off but I heard some sort of squealing noise that was getting louder and louder. At first I thought the HVAC fan seized. But, it wasn't. It was coming from Peter's office."

Avoiding eye contact, Logan took a sip of his coffee while Nicole anxiously waited for him to continue.

Logan took a deep breath and exhaled. "I walked past Peter's office. His door was open. I peered inside for a brief moment." His eyes widened, took another deep breath and exhaled. "At first I couldn't comprehend what I saw."

Nicole flipped the page, licked her pen tip, and continued writing. "What then happened, what did you see?"

"I walked to the bathroom. By the time I got to the bathroom, my brain processed Anika bouncing on Peter's lap. I am not sure if they saw me, but maybe that is why you are asking me."

Shaking her head, she grilled him. "What did you see? Is there anything else? What happened after you went to the bathroom? Did you see or hear them again?"

Logan rested his coffee cup on the table and just stared at it. "I really don't want to say anything more."

"So, you are saying they were having sex?" She couldn't let this go.

Clearly distressed, he acknowledged, "Yes! Yes, they were having sex."

Nicole slumped slightly into the chair. "Thank you. I know this was difficult to talk about. Did you see or hear anything else?"

"No, I snuck back to get my things and left."

"Please do not say anything to anyone about this matter." Nicole flipped the pages back from her notepad.

He assured her. "I won't. But, there might be another person who heard or saw this too."

"Oh? You mean Daryl?"

Logan's forehead wrinkled in bewilderment, "No. After I left the bathroom, I ran into the janitor. He might have heard or seen them. Hey, listen I really just want to forget all of this. It is quite disturbing on so many levels."

She stood and confidently agreed, "Yes, it is very disturbing and certainly uncalled for! We will do something about this. Thank you again."

Logan got up and headed out the door to escape this entire conversation.

Sitting alone in the conference room, Nicole thought, "*Why is this happening?*"

⁓23⁓

MAKE MY DAY

P eter called Howard, the firm's attorney, who was in the process of finalizing Sam's termination letter.

"Hey, I know you are busy but I need you to look at our current sales office lease and see how we can get out of it within the next three to six months as well as define any penalties or other matters that I need to be aware of. Can you get that done in a week?"

"Sure. Are you planning to move the sales office?"

"I am going to look for an office near the factory."

Curiosity peaked, Howard suggested, "You know, we could expand the factory to include a sales office and have a product demonstration and showcase area."

"Right. I remember you mentioning that before. Thanks. I need to think more about it. But, yeah, to your point, we will be closing the sales office. Much of our customer service activities are going to become automated so we won't require a large staff. Also, I am making moves to restructure Pure Air to be more competitive. Having two locations has caused many problems, such as a lack of trust, poor communications, and had definitely established a forum for unhealthy politics."

"I will get what you want as well as look into expanding the factory." Howard offered as he ended the call.

Tuesday went by very quickly. Exhausted, Peter headed home. Walking into his apartment, he hung up his coat and yelled to see if Sarah was home.

Faintly, almost wistfully, she replied, "I am in the living room, looking at the skyline."

Peter walked over to her, gave her a kiss, and said, "Yes, it is a nice view" and asked if he could refill her glass of Moscato. She seemed to be in deep thought.

"No, thanks. I was just wondering. Are you still planning to fire Sam on Friday?"

Walking into the kitchen looking for a light snack before dinner, he replied, "Yes. But don't worry, I am offering her a very generous package."

Realizing what he was looking for, she called out, "There are vegetables, hummus, and some stuffed grape leaves on the counter. You can bring it in here."

Disgruntled, he cried, "What happened to the cheese platter and prosciutto?"

"That's not on the food list the doctor gave me for you to eat and you know it! What will the rest of the staff and managers think about Sam leaving?"

"They will be okay with it." Peter cautiously bit into one of the stuffed grape leaves and thought, *"This grape leaf filler kind of tastes like cheese."*

"Are there any other changes?"

Turning his attention back to Sarah, "Yeah, quite a few."

"What about Nicole? Are you thinking of advancing her?"

"I think it's time I promote her to HR director."

Sarah took a sip of wine and nodded in complete agreement. "I have been telling you that for years! You cannot lose her; she is great."

Peter swallowed the rest of the stuffed grape leaf, then took a handful of baby carrots in one hand as Sarah continued her inquisition.

"I think Nicole will make a great HR director. She is always so helpful and in tune with the staff. What about Anika?"

Peter took a bite of one carrot and spoke while crunching away. "She will be the new marketing director."

"Personally, I wouldn't move her into marketing. In fact, I would fire that witch!" she forcefully asserted.

Peter almost choked on the carrot he was still munching on. "You would fire both Sam and Anika?"

"As far as Anika goes, you know she isn't very well liked. Her staff have so many problems with her attitude. I think if you got rid of her, everyone's morale would immediately improve. And, face it, with improved morale, you get increased sales."

Peter walked back into the kitchen and threw his handful of baby carrots into the garbage can. Thinking to himself, *"Damn, I wish that doctor never gave her that food list,"* he replied to his wife's comment, "Oh, really? You really think she is that much a detriment to the culture?"

Sarah stood up and started walking to the kitchen. "Yes, I do."

Defensively, he contended, "Well, I like that she deals with the people coming in late."

Sarah now was face to face with Peter. "Honey, you need to realize times have changed. Flex hours are the way most companies are going. I think Pure Air would be better off if you allowed the staff to work out their own work schedule instead of having someone like her snitch on them."

Peter wrapped both arms around Sarah's waist. "I have something else to tell you."

Sarah thought, *"He always does this when he has a surprise."*

"I will be closing our sales office shortly and we will move back into the factory."

Expecting something completely different from him, Sarah stepped back. "Does that mean we have to move?"

"Definitely, it is too far to commute."

Considering his idea, she smiled. "Well, I support you in whatever you decide."

Peter took a few steps forward and put his hands back on her waist. "Are you okay with moving?"

"Yeah, I think I am okay with it. I know you need to make changes and having everyone in one place will help out a lot."

"Good. I thought you might see it that way. And you can start looking for houses."

Snuggling into his embrace, she relaxed. "This will be a new chapter for us to start."

"A better chapter." Peter leaned down and kissed the top of her head before squeezing her tighter.

Wednesday, Peter called Nicole into his office. She had a pile of papers for Peter to sign when she walked in and placed them in front of him, nearly spilling his coffee on his desk. She inquisitively chirped, "Seems there are a lot of things going around here."

Slightly baffled by her statement, he tipped his head and asked, "What do you mean?"

"Well, you must know that having Logan come on board has really stirred the pot."

As if not hearing her, Peter signed the remaining documents and paused. "So I am just curious. Why didn't you apply for the HR Manager position at the factory?"

Taken back by his question, "Basically, I really don't want to make a lateral move, and it would mean I would report to Steve. I prefer to report to you."

Peter mischievously smiled. "What if the position was a director level and still reported to me?"

"If it was a director role and I reported to you, then of course I would accept it."

Without looking up from the documents. "All right, then, write up a job description for HR director."

Nicole stopped in her tracks. "What? Really? Great! I will get that right to you. Thanks."

Peter took off his reading glasses and placed them on the desk. "You do know you would have to move to the factory, right?"

Nicole's eyebrows raised. "I am fine with moving there, but there are some moving expenses that I can't afford at the moment."

"Don't worry. I will cover your moving expenses. We can discuss the details later."

Still off balance from everything, she continued. "But, I don't know how much it will cost. And, I have a rental contract."

"Send your rental agreement to Howard. He can look it over. What else?" Peter grabbed his glasses and held them ready to put on.

"Um, nothing. My daughter can transfer to a school there. I am sure it will be better for her and for me."

"Ok, so it's done. New position, new work location, new school, new apartment, right?

"Wow, really? Yes. Yes, of course. Thanks! You just made my day."

Peter handed Nicole the folders. "I know Steve is looking forward to having you at the factory. Before we make this official, please post the HR director position in the sales office and factory."

Gleefully, Nicole gleefully declared, "Absolutely. I will get that done immediately. Thanks again Peter."

"No problem. You deserve it, Nicole."

-24-

SHAKE, RATTLE, AND ROLL

L ogan walked into Peter's office to check in and suggest strategic organizational changes. "Logan, your
contract is about to end this month, tell me why I should
renew it?" Peter held a document in his hand and started
to read it.

Without faltering at the unexpected question, "Well, I have
implemented several process changes that are improving
the productivity of your customer service team. Daryl can
verify this with the financials. Also, I continually identify
issues and take actions to improve things."

Peter put down the document, took off his cheaters, and
set them on the papers. "Yeah, well, I suppose you could
do it faster."

"Well, I suppose I could for some things, but I am certain
that would cause more problems."

"Think about it, then do it. I am going to renew your contract for another 12 months. I want to keep you on retainer
to advise my team as they take over the implementation

of the changes. I am thinking you work full-time, spend more time with Steve and his team at the factory until we move things down there. Then, we can trim down your time to part-time or on a project-by-project basis."

Agreeing with Peter's decision, "Fine, let's amend the contract stating that and we can make a timeline once the organizational changes are made and the sales office moves."

Peter slid the document he had been reading across the desk. "Go ahead and update it. By the way, Steve called me and said he very much appreciated your candor at the factory. I think you and he will work great together. He wants you back at the factory soon."

"Sure. I will make the changes and get it back to you later."

With insight, Peter mused, "You know, I thought I had the right team until I met with you and before we visited the factory together. Getting the right team is now my first priority."

Logan folded the contract and stuffed it into his planner. "We still need to spend time mapping out strategies, especially from an organizational perspective with individual performance metrics."

"Next week we can start that. Let's keep it at a 30,000-foot level. Why don't you go ahead and update your contract and start developing a strategic map."

The next morning, Nicole was in her office early and was much more cheerful than normal. She had brought in fancy cupcakes that she usually reserved for holidays. Bob stopped by Nicole's desk. "Want a cupcake?"

"Sure. What's going on with you? Seems like you are much happier than normal. In fact, it seems several people here are much happier. I need to get my hands on some of that Kool-Aid you guys drank." Conspiratorially, he leaned in closer to Nicole and whispered, "Last night I saw a new job posting for a HR Director. I suppose you already got the position."

She quickly glanced around to make sure no one else overheard him. "Hush. It is not official yet."

"Congratulations!" He winked, took one of the cupcakes and walked away smiling.

Anika was noticeably vacant from her sentry post and spent the entire morning at her desk. The staff were relieved not to have someone constantly walking around checking their work and monitoring their calls.

As he passed by Nicole's desk mid-morning, Peter instructed her, "Please come to my office."

Nicole got up and followed him. Peter noticed cupcakes on her desk and chuckled, "It seems you are already celebrating."

Turning pink, she giggled, "Actually, we celebrated at home last night. It's fun making cupcakes, too."

Once they arrived in his office, Peter closed the door. "Can you stay tomorrow until 6pm?"

"Sure! Why, what's up?"

"As you know there are some changes taking place. I am moving Pure Air in a better and leaner direction with more accountability. I am terminating Sam's employment and will need to have you sit in on the meeting as well as have the checklist available for her to turn in her laptop and phone."

Nicole's eyes opened wide. "Wow! That came from left field. I was not expecting that at all."

"Get ready to jump into your new role. There will be more organization changes coming up as well as new ways of doing things."

Excited, she nodded. "I get that."

"Can you also find a few boxes for Sam's things but keep that discreet."

"Sure and I will keep them out of sight until Friday evening."

"Thanks! See you later."

Friday started on a similar note as Thursday except without cupcakes. Peter and Daryl spent most of the morning together in Peter's office while Sam spent her morning in her office. Peter texted Sam, "Can you meet later today?"

"Sure, what time?"

"5pm."

Peter printed two copies of the termination letter with all of the severance package details and put them into two folders. Daryl said, "Good luck" then walked out of Peter's office.

Peter had spent the last hour or so contemplating the discussion with Sam when Sarah called. "I just want to say good luck. I know it will be difficult but it will go smoothly."

He agreed with her sentiment. "I am sure there won't be any problems. See you tonight."

Logan was meeting with several staff and happened to see Sam. "Do you have time to meet?"

"Not today but how about Monday?"

"Perfect. Let me know what time is best for you."

As the clock ticked closer to 5pm, everyone was getting ready to leave for the weekend. Nicole was still at her desk when she saw Sam walk toward Peter's office. She got up just as Sam knocked on Peter's door and he announced "Come in, please sit down."

Nicole followed suit and he asked her to sit down as well.

Sam's nerves prickled when Nicole sat down next to her. Taking a deep breath, Peter looked at Sam and began as if he had practiced a speech. "I am just going to come out and say this directly. I very much appreciate your service here. But, I am taking Pure Air in a different direction. Here is a termination letter I would like you to sign. I have included a generous severance package if you resign effective immediately."

"What? Really? Why?" Sam's eyes began to water. "This is totally unexpected. I know we have been in a slump, but we can get out of it together." As one tear rolled down her cheek, she slowly reached out, clutched the letter, and began reading.

Peter watched solemnly as Nicole slid a box of tissues to Sam. It felt like for the first time, he thought of Samantha as a person with feelings and emotions. She was always so strong, determined, and capable.

Gathering himself, Peter continued, "Basically, the severance package includes your salary, medical, bonus, and commissions paid through the end of this year. Also, there are other perks we will continue to pay too. I would like you to accept this now without any edits."

Overwhelmed with a tidal wave of shock, she choked out, "I don't think this is the right thing to do. I was not expecting this at all. I am surprised. I am really shocked and, to be honest, I am horribly disappointed." Sam lifted a tissue to the corner of her eyes, then patted her face with it.

Filled with emotion, Nicole grabbed a tissue and touched her own eyes before the tears started to roll. The reality overwhelmed Peter as his eyes started to tear as well.

With a lump in his throat, Peter asked, "Nicole, do you have the checklist?" She handed him the checklist and he placed it in front of Sam. "Please take the checklist and complete this with Nicole tonight. We will need your laptop and password, and phone and password."

Sam sat there for a long minute, silent and red-faced, her hands shaking.

After what seemed a millennium, she said, "Ok, so, what is the next step? When do you need my laptop and phone?"

Realizing she hadn't comprehended his statement, he gently repeated, "We will need your laptop and phone tonight." Nicole has some boxes that you can put your things in. She can help pack too."

Sam got up, extended her hand crisply and firmly. Peter stood up and shook her hand. "Thank you Sam for your understanding, and your professionalism."

Sam's face was red and still stunned by what just happened. Without a word, she turned slowly, and walked out with her dignity intact and Nicole followed. She walked into her office for the last time and stood there dazed. That is when she realized Nicole was beside her. Sam handed over her laptop and phone.

Nicole quietly asked, "Can you write down your passwords?" Sam was a little distracted and fumbled with a few things on top of her desk. "Here you go. Here is a list of all the programs with my passwords. Oh, wait. Let me write down my phone password on here."

Showing her own emotions and hoping to give Sam some comfort, Nicole put the paper in her pocket and offered, "Thanks. Here, let me help you with your things." Both women resisted the urge to hug.

"How many boxes do you need? Let me go get a couple now and if you need more, I can get them."

Still in a fog, Sam mumbled, "Fine. Probably one or two is fine."

When Nicole returned with some boxes, she saw a bunch of things were already stacked on top of the desk as Sam continued to empty out the drawers.

Nicole began carefully placing the items into the boxes. Sam looked up trying not to let the tears flow. "Thanks, I appreciate you helping me do this."

Keeping her own voice steady, she gently prompted, "It is no problem. I am here to help."

"Yeah, well, thanks."

Nicole topped off one box with a lid. "I think we can put everything else into the other box. I have a cart at my desk we can put them on and I will help bring them to your car."

Sam felt a moment of relief and tried to smile, "Thanks again, Nicole. You are so kind."

Choking up, she swallowed. "Thanks, Sam. I'm sorry it has to be this way. To be honest, I was kind of surprised. But, that's not my decision. And you could see it was not easy for Peter. It really wasn't."

"I suppose so, Nicole. I can't believe it. I'm in shock. I don't know what I'm going to do."

Reassuring her, she asserted, "You're talented. Believe me, you'll land on your feet and find greater success elsewhere. I know you are probably feeling a huge range of emotions right now. Promise me you will take advantage of the outplacement services included in the package."

"I appreciate the vote of confidence and I promise I will. This is just hard right now."

Turning to retrieve the cart from her office, she nodded. "I understand."

Sam looked around her office for the last time as she loaded the cart.

Nicole pushed the cart toward the lobby while Sam stopped at Peter's doorway. "See you."

Peter looked up and said with an upbeat voice, "Good luck and thank you for your work here."

"By the way, what will you say to the customers and others when they ask what happened with me?"

Smiling, he assured her, "I will say you left on good terms and that I really don't know where you went."

Stumbling for words, she meekly smiled. "I appreciate that. It's hard, Peter. I don't know what to say. I guess, goodbye, and good luck to you and the company."

After helping Sam pack her car and saying their goodbyes, Nicole went back to Peter's office. "What's next?"

"Please finish the termination checklist yourself. Next week, I will send out a letter informing our customers and make an internal announcement about Sam. Next week, I'll have you make a few more job description changes, but no more terminations."

"That's good to hear! Have a nice weekend and I'll see you Monday."

Monday started normally with most everyone in Anika's 9am meeting. Halfway through the meeting, everyone received a text message about Sam's departure. Also, all of the sales reps and others outside the company received an email blast about Sam's interest to pursue other opportunities and a thank you note for her service.

Anika stopped talking when the phones buzzed and beeped. Suddenly, there were several gasps and a surprised look on everyone's faces. Instead of looking at her phone, she looked around the room. She instantly knew something was up. Only then did she grab her phone and saw the announcement. Abruptly, she announced, "I think we can end the meeting; thanks." She slammed her laptop and notepad, stood up, and raced to Peter's office.

Anika burst into Peter's office despite him being on the phone. He looked up, waved his hand to have her come in. Anika sat there impatiently shifting herself in the chair as Peter turned sideways so he could not see her and continued talking. Perturbed at being ignored, Anika leaned in his direction, tilted her head, and said, "We need to talk."

Clearly annoyed, Peter covered the phone receiver with one hand, then sternly said, "In a moment."

As soon as Peter hung up the phone, she pounced. "That was a surprising move!"

Ignoring what she just said, he asked, "Have you thought more about the marketing director position?"

"Yes, you said I have until the end of the week to make plans and make a budget."

"I know I did but I need to keep things moving. Will you accept the marketing director role along with a $10,000 pay increase?"

"Certainly. I can start immediately but I have so many staff to manage."

"Let's talk about that later, I have other calls to make. Is there anything else?"

"Well, yes," she began. "I didn't know that Sam—" She stopped herself. "No, nothing at all." She stood up and left. She thought, *"A $10,000 increase is pretty good. I wanted to talk about Sam's departure, but it was obvious he wouldn't discuss it. It's too late to go back in there. Did he do that on purpose?"*

As Anika left, Peter called Bob into his office. Eager to hear directly from Peter about Sam's departure, he hurried over. Without any preamble, Peter began, "Thanks for coming in so fast. Hey, listen, I need us to be more focused on increasing sales and margins. I want you to take the lead on all commercial sales along with having some of the customer service staff report directly to you."

Stumped by the direction of the conversation, Bob merely said, "Umm, ok, sounds great. But, what will happen to Anika?" He forgot to mention Sam.

"I am moving her to the director of marketing position. I am naming you director of commercial sales and Kevin will be director of residential sales. I think he is ready but will still need your help. Do you think you can do that but give him latitude to run his own show?"

"Sure! I think that's a great move."

"Good, please go get Kevin." Happy to hear this good news, he all but ran to Kevin and said, "Hey, buddy, follow me!"

A few minutes later both newly appointed directors walked into Peter's office. By now, many of the staff were texting each other because they watched Anika walk in and out of Peter's office, then Bob, now Bob and Kevin together. A few others were on the phone whispering to each other conjuring up new rumors.

Kevin walked in and thought, *"I have been working hard. Why are they going to fire me?"*

Peter jumped right in. "Hey listen Kevin. You have been doing some good work here and I would like to offer you more responsibility."

Kevin sat up in his chair, relieved and excited. "I am ready for more responsibility!"

"Good. I am promoting you to be the director of residential sales along with supervising a group of customer service staff." Peter reached over his desk extending his hand for Kevin to shake.

Kevin jumped to his feet, bowed over the desk and shook Peter's hand vigorously. "Thanks. Thank you very much!"

As Bob and Kevin stood smiling at each other, Peter called Anika and instructed, "Please come to my office."

"In a few minutes. I have something to do."

Peter pulled his phone away from his ear and looked at his phone in a strange way. "I would really appreciate it if you come here now." Then he dropped the handset into the phone base with some extra force.

Bob and Kevin were startled by the noise and they were afraid to look at Peter.

Peter stood waiting next to his cabinet contemplating a coffee or whiskey. Bob and Kevin stood to the side of Peter's desk. Anika walked in and spit out, "So, what is so urgent?"

Turning to her, he calmly stated, "Each of you now has a new role. Anika, your staff will be divided up and they will report to either Bob or Kevin. You can have a couple staff to support your new marketing department. I prefer you to form your team from our current staff. I expect the three of you to define your new team by the end of today. After you agree on your teams, send me the list for review and approval. I will then send out an announcement. Are we clear?"

Bob looked at Kevin, then at Anika, "Let's go out to lunch and work off-site until this is done."

Anika sullenly reported, "Sorry, I have other plans."

Looking stern, Peter barked. "You need to cancel them."

She thought about protesting for a millisecond and decided to go with it "Fine, I will make a schedule change. We will do lunch and work out the details."

"I am all for getting this done today. I can organize a list with all the customer service staff." Kevin eagerly waited for someone to say the next action.

"Don't forget about the remote workers and technicians" Peter added. He then decided to hell with it, and grabbed the whiskey.

Bob said, "Who do the sales reps report to?"

Opening the bottle and pouring himself a good amount of the nerve-calming liquid, Peter responded, "the sales reps and technicians will report to either of you two." He put down the bottle and pointed to Bob and Kevin.

Anika looked at Bob, Kevin, and then stared at Peter. With emphasis, she blurted "Seriously? I think these two will struggle trying to manage the staff!" She talked to Peter as though Bob and Kevin were not there. "I am willing to try this new way for a short time, and then re-evaluate. If there are issues, you and I should be able to come up with a new plan."

Peter ignored her last comment and commanded, "If there isn't anything else, go get your lunch and work out the details. I will want to review the details tomorrow morning. See you tomorrow." Sending a clear message they were done with the meeting, he pulled out his chair, sat down, held up his whiskey, checked the glass to be sure he had poured himself enough and took a short sip.

Anika, Bob, and Kevin left the office unable to hide their astonishment. Bob and Kevin didn't agree with how Anika talked to Peter, but neither said anything to her. Anika was furious that all of her team was cut out from under her. She thought to herself as she stewed, *"In one month's time, I will find a way to get rid of these two and have my staff back!"*

"There is a tavern across the street. We can have the upstairs room all to ourselves" suggested Bob.

"I will meet you there shortly. I have to cancel my other plans. Order me a salad." Anika ordered as she headed into her office.

In unison, both men sarcastically responded "Sure thing!" and walked toward the exit.

As soon as the three left his office, Peter called Steve and told him about the upcoming changes.

Sounding excited, Steve responded, "Great idea of splitting off the sales groups. They are really two different product lines and this allows each group to be better focused. Honestly, I am not sure about Anika as the marketing director. But, she might be able to do it." He never approached the subject of Sam's departure.

"You know I promoted Nicole as the HR director. She will be responsible for the sales office and factory."

"Yeah, you told me. I think it is great; she will do an incredible job!"

Peter continued, "One other thing. We are upgrading our website so customers can order directly online. The website will have tools along with an automated support assistant. Eventually, we might only need a handful of customer service staff. This will take some time to implement, including moving the sales office into the factory. I am sure we will lose people because of organization changes, the sales office move, and general attrition."

Thrilled at the changes, Steve jibed him. "So you finally decided on moving to the factory?"

"I am thinking we expand the factory to house the sales team but also, and more importantly, to build a product demonstration area."

"Nice! I like this a lot. Looking forward to everything changing for the better."

Grateful for Steve's reaction, Peter concluded, "All right. I figured I would give you a quick call and update you, thanks."

Peter hung up the phone and muttered almost inaudibly to the empty office, "Damn it! This all better work out or I'll be drinking a quart a day, firing Logan, cashing in my stock, and moving to Aruba."

~25~

HORSE TRADING

Bob, Kevin, and Anika were discussing the new changes for themselves while eating upstairs at the tavern. Anika arrogantly said, "I am glad I will have time to make new strategies for Pure Air."

Ignoring her tone, Bob piped in. "I think it is finally time to separate commercial from residential. Kevin and I already separate upcoming projects this way."

"I like residential products more than commercial, so I think all of us got what we wanted. Except the staff; they may not like the split. How are we going to divide up the staff? I think we should have invited Nicole."

"No! We can do this without her. I can separate the staff by myself," snapped Anika.

Kevin continued, "Ouch! That's kind of harsh. But I guess we don't need to involve HR right now. Nicole would want to bring up each person's file, review their competency, previous personnel review, career interests, and maybe even their attendance record. It would take days just to set up the teams."

Bob looked at Kevin with some concern. "Ok. But, who will coordinate this with her?"

Kevin waved his hand through the air as if to chase his concerns away. "All we need to do is provide Peter with the list of names. He will work with Nicole to get the rest of the paperwork completed."

"Are we ready to do this now?" Anika was clearly getting annoyed as she finished her salad.

Both men nodded in agreement. "Yeah, sure."

Anika took charge and announced, "The call volume is definitely greater for commercial than residential and there are many customers that call for commercial parts."

Bob interrupted her and suggested, "Let's start with marketing. Who do you want on your team?"

"I want Roman to help me build the new website."

Kevin nodded in agreement and moved Roman's name under Anika's name on the spreadsheet. "That is a good choice, I agree," "What marketing strategies have you and Peter discussed?"

Anika continued identifying her needs. "Several are analytical in nature so I will need one or two people to be able to extract, compile, analyze, organize, and report various datasets."

Jokingly, Kevin said, "Well, that sounds like a job for me." She made it clear she didn't find that humorous at all.

Bob laughed, "In your spare time you could help but she needs someone fulltime."

Glaring at them, she spouted, "Come on guys, I am serious. I want to take both Juanita and Daven" as she looked at Bob.

"Those are good choices. They work well together."

"Daven is not that good with analyzing data. He makes many mistakes and I always have to correct him." Kevin moved those names to her team.

Refusing to budge on her choices, Anika argued, "Well that will be my problem won't it! Do you have any other concern?"

Kevin sat silently not wanting her to get angrier. Bob broke the uncomfortable silence. "OK, so that rounds out the marketing team."

"Wait a second. I might want one more person!"

Determined to ensure Kevin and he had a say in the way things were divided, Bob interrupted, "Hold that point. Let's decide on a way to divide the group. At the end, we may see a way to move one more person into marketing."

"I suggest we make a matrix with factors such as commercial skill level A, B, C where A is very knowledgeable and C has basic understanding. Also, we can add work shift times, remote work or in office work," said Kevin.

Shaking his head, Bob continued, "I don't think we need to judge each staff. I think we can just go through the names and assign them accordingly."

Anika nodded in agreement. So Kevin turned his screen showing the spreadsheet. "Here is the list of the staff names. I already moved the people Anika wants."

Anika stood while Bob leaned in to see Kevin's screen. "Hold on one second. The projector is in my briefcase."

"I've got my staff, I don't care how you split the rest." She took another step away from them.

Kevin turned on the projector and a list of names appeared. Beside the names, there were columns next to each of their names. Only Anika's column contained names.

Kevin read one name and Bob raised his hand "Me." Kevin continued to call out several names with Bob claiming each of them. On the next name, Kevin smiled when Bob chirped, "You."

He didn't challenge Bob's choices until several more names went to Bob's column.

Scowling, Kevin interrupted. "So far it seems all the competent people are going to commercial. I need to have a couple good ones too!"

"I agree, you can have Maria and Regina, but I keep Natalie."

"l am going to highlight Maria because I think she should also be in residential."

"OK". Kevin continued sounding off names.

Anika was paying more attention to moving her olives and croutons aside in her bowl than to the conversation.

Barely an hour passed since eating lunch when the list was finalized. Surprised, Anika announced, "I thought this horse trading was going to take a lot longer."

"Kevin and I have a great working relationship. We both accept that if we need to make a change a week later, then we will just move staff or change the workload differently."

She glared at them and shook her finger in shame. "You shouldn't treat people like objects."

Bob laughed as he thought, *"That's exactly how you treat people."* But, he kept that thought to himself because as she would be offended and never let him forget.

Kevin was always acquiescing to Anika. He feigned blindness and hearing loss when she berated her staff and always avoided a direct argument with her.

Anika stood and firmly informed them, "Seems the list is finished except I may want one more staff. I will discuss this with Peter later."

Kevin immediately looked troubled. "Oops. I just emailed Peter the list and copied you. I didn't think he wanted to meet with us. He just said to send it and he would review it and decide if the list makes sense or not." Turning to Bob for support, he hesitantly looked at Anika.

Anika flipped her hair over her shoulder as she turned to leave. "I will meet with him later anyway, so don't worry about it."

Kevin exhaled and slouched in his chair after she walked out. Bob waited for Kevin to pack up his stuff and they walked back to the office together.

For the next two days, Peter and Anika met continually to hash out the marketing strategy, website improvements, budget, KPIs, and various other things.

Logan tried to meet with Peter to show him the updates to the SIOPP workshop. However, Peter believed any change would be an improvement and had no intention of wasting time with Logan.

Bob and Kevin conducted their work as if nothing happened. They were waiting for Peter to announce the organizational changes. Several staff tried to have private discussions with Bob or Kevin to find out what was going on but were unable to pry any information from them. Bob and Kevin just kept telling them that a real positive change would be announced shortly.

As days went by, office morale decayed further. More rumors floated around. Staff openly worked on their resume or were on calls with recruiters. One staff heard from a friend that the sales office lease was going to be terminated. That rumor was openly discussed in meetings and in the hallways.

Eventually Nicole caught wind of it. She listened but didn't have a response. Believing Peter should be fielding these questions directly, she texted Peter for the third time this week, "You need to make the announcement. Office morale is really bad."

─26─

GENEROUS DICTATOR

Peter called Logan into his office. As Logan walked through the customer service cubicles, he observed scowls, whispers, and furtive, nervous movements. He had heard one rumor that Pure Air was being sold; another rumor was that Steve was the new General Manager and that he was going to close the sales office. As Logan passed by Nicole's office, Nicole waved him over to her desk.

She whispered, "Are you going to see Peter?"

"Yeah, what's up?"

"Please convince him to have a town hall meeting with the customer service team soon. Everyone wants to hear Peter talk about Pure Air's future. The morale is declining rapidly."

"Yeah, I get the same feeling. I'll see what I can do."

Logan walked into Peter's office and saw many large sheets of paper taped to the walls. The paper sheets had notes, diagrams, numbers, competitor names; it looked as though Peter's brain was dissected with information and thrown haphazardly on the wall.

Without looking away from the papers, Peter sensed Logan's arrival and said, "I have been busy with Anika developing marketing plans. I want to show you the new organization." Peter walked over to his desk and searched for the chart.

Logan still looking at the artwork on the wall. "How are things now that Samantha has departed?"

"Listen, I don't want to talk about that." Peter's phone buzzed, then a few seconds later buzzed again. "Seems as though every customer wants to speak with me now that Sam has left. Take a look at the new organization chart." Peter reached out with a print out.

Logan looked at the chart and said, "Looks like you are implementing what we talked about during our factory trip. I see you have completely removed all of the customer service staff from Anika and put them under Bob or Kevin. I think that is a good thing, especially if you want to promote a culture change. The SIOPP tool will work much better this way too.

Distracted, Peter mumbled, "Remind me again; what is the SIOPP tool?"

Logan placed the chart on Peter's desk. "It is a weekly meeting your Sales, Operations, Supply Chain, and

Finance teams hold to agree on the Sales, Inventory, Operations, Planning, and Purchasing activities for the next 12 weeks."

"Right. I remember you saying that."

"Promoting Nicole was a no brainer. I would have thought this would have been done a long time ago. Are there accompanying strategies and performance metrics for each manager?" Logan walked closer to Peter.

Peter was staring at his notes on the wall. "I have put together strategies and metrics for everyone except Anika. I have been working with her over the past few days." He shifted his look from Logan to his whiskey cabinet.

Logan tried to follow the logic on the wall but it was too haphazard. "Well, I think when you give more responsibility, you should also give them higher expectations."

"Noted. So, I just wanted to show you the new organization before it is communicated to the managers and at the town hall meetings."

"When will you announce the new organization, and have you thought through all the questions the staff will ask?"

Peter walked behind his desk, rolled back and sat in his lavish, ergonomic chair. "Soon, very soon. The staff will like this change a lot. Thanks for your help."

"What about the rumors?"

Peter's confidence showed. He folded his hands together. "I am not worried about rumors. Can you ask Nicole to come see me?"

Logan walked out and thought with a grin, *"The staff will like this a lot. They won't be hounded by Anika any longer."*

Nicole entered Peter's office. "Hi Nicole, would you schedule three town hall meetings, one in the sales office, one in the factory, and a teleconference one for the remote workers?"

Nicole didn't answer right away. She thought, *"We need an admin person. I got promoted in title and demoted in work responsibility."* "Sure, I can do that." She wrote in her daily planner, *"Admin needed"* as she stood in place.

Peter looked confused. "Is there something else to talk about?"

"Well, I suggest you address the rumors. I have told you many times the morale is bitterly low."

"Don't worry. Things will change for the better very soon."

Nicole circled the admin role a few times in her planner and thought out loud. "Tomorrow we should have the customer service town hall meeting, first thing in the morning."

Peter sensed something else was bothering her. "By the way, take a look at the new organization chart." Peter swiveled his desktop screen.

"This is a huge change. Am I the last to know?" she asked bitterly.

"What do you mean?"

"Well, it seems I am nearly always the last to know here and I am the HR Director."

Holding up his hands to stop her, Peter spouted, "Wait a minute. I never meant to exclude you. Seems like you are being overly sensitive."

"It is just frustrating when I hear someone has been hired or someone is reporting to another person, or even when you say you are giving a bonus or pay increase. Would you mind bringing me in earlier on these changes? I am sure I can help. Plus, it's my job, after all."

Peter tapped his pen on a notepad. "I suppose I do take you for granted, but you have been with me for years. We all need to make changes. I will try to get you involved earlier."

Nicole saw her chance. "I hope so. Oh, and by the way, we need an admin person to help with things around here. I just can't keep taking work home at night."

"Why are you just telling me this now?"

"I don't know, things have been going a little crazy. I am way behind with work and do not see how I can catch up."

"I will call Steve and see if he can do something about it."

Surprised and somewhat pleased at the quick solution, she asked, "Why would Steve need to be involved?"

"Because your admin will have to be located at the factory. Perhaps Steve already has one. Don't worry, we will work something out."

"I appreciate that. Are there new job descriptions for the role changes? And, are there any salary changes, or any other changes?"

"I will email you the organization chart and I will summarize the changes so you can do the appropriate updates."

"Thanks. I can draft the organization announcement." Nicole started to write in her planner.

"Don't worry. I can write it up."

"With all due respect, Peter, now that I am the HR Director, that's my responsibility."

"Ok, fine. I was just trying to help with your workload." Peter put his pen down.

"I suggest you have a meeting with the managers today about their new roles before you make an announcement."

"Good idea. Let's do that today. I want the managers to be more engaged and be more accountable. I am going to try to be less of a dictator."

Nicole brought her hand up to her mouth, holding her laugh, then jokingly said, "You mean you are giving up the throne almighty?"

Peter knew she was joking, so he played along. "I am a kind and generous dictator."

Nicole actually laughed out loud. "Oh, yes you are. You are that and a lot more."

"Since you are so happy, would you arrange lunch for the managers today?"

"Sure." She left his office with a cheery smile and bounce.

At noon, Bob, Kevin, and Daryl walked into the conference room together and started to load their plates with the catered food. Steve called in on videoconference and was eating lunch at his desk. Anika walked in just after Daryl sat down, then Peter and Nicole lined up behind Anika.

Peter started a speech while putting food on his plate. "Today marks a new day for our company. I am very proud to have all of you represent Pure Air. You are now the new face of our company. Together you will define strategies and metrics. This change will make us more competitive, responsive, and have you more engaged and accountable."

No one responded to Peter's speech; he hadn't really expected any response.

Steve was talking but no one could hear him. Nicole said, "Steve, we cannot hear you. Unmute yourself."

Steve unmuted then repeated, "I like this change. This should reduce the politics and rumors. There is one thing I would like us to do. As a summary of our meeting, we should define the key points so we can address the same message to our staff."

Bob said, "I think having us define meeting points is very helpful. Also, I think we should define an executive accord. It should be a list of actions that all of us will comply with all of the time."

Anika butted in. "Guys, we have different personalities, different responsibilities, and different metrics. Do you seriously think we will agree on a certain strategy? Does a majority win?"

"This sounds like more bureaucracy. What happens when one or more of us fails to meet one of the accords or has multiple violations to an accord? See?" said Daryl as he slid his plate behind his laptop. He opened it and started typing.

Peter halted their discussion. "Listen, each of you are an executive and each of you should make decisions based on the needs of the business, not the needs or wishes of you or your function. I am going to leave this in your hands to figure out. Peter looked around the room and then left."

Anika waved goodbye. There was silence and everyone stared at each other.

"Excuse me. Hello? Can you hear me? Hey, I am having trouble hearing you. Please be close to the microphone when talking. Can we get back to discussing an accord?"

"I am not going to work on any accord. I suggest we discuss and prioritize strategies and metrics," huffed Anika.

Bob and Nicole eyed each other while Kevin remained silent. He didn't know what to say. Daryl was locked deep into his spreadsheet algorithm.

Not getting any replies from the group, Steve repeated, "Guys, can you hear me? I don't know if you can hear me."

Anika finally barked, "Steve, we can hear you just fine. Is everyone prepared to discuss strategies and metrics? If not, then we should schedule a meeting."

Nicole pushed back her chair, offended by Anika's rudeness. "You aren't the leader here."

Bob held up his hands, "I think we all need a day to accept these new changes. I will schedule a meeting tomorrow afternoon. Steve, is it possible for you to come here?"

"Yeah, see you tomorrow. Thanks Bob for coordinating."
Steve turned off his video.

"I suggest everyone come prepared for the next meeting."
Anika sneered as she got up and left.

Bob, Nicole, and Kevin got up and started to leave. Bob
realized Daryl hadn't moved. "Hey, Daryl! The meeting is
over."

Daryl's eyes didn't leave his screen. He just waved goodbye.

–27–

Just the Facts

Peter was on the phone when Nicole walked in. She stomped up to his desk holding a notepad in one hand and a pen in the other. Peter raised his finger and lightly kissed it indicating he needed her to be quiet so he could finish his call. Barely able to contain herself, she tapped the floor with her toe and harshly clicked her pen.

Patience completely exhausted, she blurted, "We need to talk and we need to talk right now."

Peter was intently listening on the phone so he didn't hear Nicole's words. He did sense it was important and urgent so he concluded his conversation. "That's at least some good news. So, my next appointment is in two days, right? See you then."

Just as Peter's handset touched the phone base, Nicole shot out, "We need to have a talk."

"Ok, hold on one second while I write this down. You know I forget things easily." Peter finished writing, put down his pen, and cheerfully asked, "So, how I can help you today?"

"This is no time to smile. You have made a serious judgment error and I want to hear it directly from you."

Peter looked perplexed. "So, what's this about?"

"Last Wednesday night. I want to hear about what happened last Wednesday night."

Peter brought his hand up to his chin, then scratched his face. "Let me think."

So angry and almost shouting, "What do you mean 'let me think?' Tell me about Anika being in your office!"

His face changed from bewilderment to embarrassment and he could hear his pulse ricocheting in his ears. "I need a drink first." Peter got up and walked over to his cabinet. On the way, he thought, "*I should tell her and Sarah the truth. Otherwise, I will lose everything. Shit! I might lose everything anyway.*"

Nicole snapped him out of his thoughts. "Go ahead and pour yourself a good helping. You're going to need it."

Peter grabbed a single malt whiskey and poured a glass. He stood there, looked at it, smelled the aroma, and took his first among many swallows before he finally spoke. "Listen. I will tell you exactly what happened. But, it didn't start last Wednesday."

Trying to control her rage, Nicole flipped open her notepad to a fresh page.

Peter took a sip, swished it around his mouth, swallowed a tiny bit and swished again. "A few weeks ago, Anika started flirting with me. At first, I didn't know what to make of it. Truthfully, I didn't even realize she was flirting. But, I soon caught on, especially when she touched and stroked my hand one day. Then, on another day, she approached me and stood facing me. She grabbed both my hands and put them on her waist. I was in shock and didn't move at first."

Nicole shook her head in disgust as she stared at words she had written.

He looked at Nicole and attempted to defend himself. "I stepped back. Honest, I wasn't interested in what she wanted!" Almost pleading, he continued. "It's true. I still don't get it. But she kept flirting and I caved. She is quite attractive when she wants to be."

Peter paced back and forth in front of his cabinet. He downed a bigger helping of the amber liquid, then inhaled deeply through his puckered face. "Over the course of the next week or so, it pretty much more of the same. She would flirt, then tease, then try to entertain me. I stopped her. Well, I stopped her mostly."

Nicole flipped a page and encouraged him to continue. "You are brave to say this honestly. Please keep going. But first answer me one thing, Peter. How could you? What got into you?"

More sheepishly, he forged on. "Last Wednesday, her flirting went out of control. I was having a bad day. At the end of the day, I lost an account, so I was contemplating a recovery plan while having some whiskey. Anika walked in and as usual I wasn't interested. But, within minutes, we were, um she was... oh Christ, the next thing I knew she was bouncing on my lap. I wasn't thinking at all. It just happened." Hanging his head in shame, he stopped and downed the last of the liquor.

"All right, all right. Got it. Did you tell Sarah any of this?"

"No! Well, sort of, yes. No, not the details anyway," he stammered.

Throwing her shoulders back, she said with indignation, "Well, you need to tell her all the details. I am not a marriage counselor, but you need to be open and honest with her. Damn it Peter! You know how close Sarah and I are."

Pacing incessantly, his shoulders drooped in remorse, he murmured, "You are right, she needs to know." He poured another shot and drained the glass once more.

"How many times have you had sex with her?"

"Just that once."

"Is that the truth?"

Peter stopped walking and looked at her squarely. "Yes, only one time."

"Listen, I want all the facts. This needs to be documented

completely, then we will meet with Howard. The attorneys need to get involved."

"I get it. This is embarrassing, upsetting, immature, irresponsible, and worst of all, unfaithful!"

He put the glass on the cabinet shelf next to the half-empty whiskey bottle, feeling contrite and ashamed.

"And don't you dare drive home! You better call an Uber®" she shot as she walked out.

~28~

THE SHOCKER

"What's the matter? Aren't you feeling well?" Sarah sat across the dinner table from Peter.

Peter's forehead was sweating and his nerves were jumping. He looked at the table, "I-I-I."

"The doctor called you, right?"

"I have something to tell you."

Sarah reached across the table and laid her hand on top of Peter's hand. "Go ahead and tell me."

"It's not like that at all. I have made a grave misjudgment and I am truly sorry."

Sarah removed her hand from Peter's and placed both her hands in front of her on the table. "Go ahead and tell me."

Peter looked at her loving face then at the salt and pepper shaker. "I don't know how to say this. I am sorry. I am truly sorry."

"What the hell did you do?" Sarah's voice lost all empathy. She was furious.

Feeling like he swallowed sandpaper, he croaked, "I don't know how it happened but it did." Peter reached over the table to hold Sarah's hands, but she pushed her chair away from the table.

"What? Just tell me."

The jazz music in the other room abruptly ended. There was an awkward silence. Peter never in his mind thought of hurting Sarah. He blurted and babbled, "I was tempted by Anika and one time last week, we-we-we had sex."

"You what? You were tempted? What? Her? Why? You son of a bitch!" Sarah screamed as the tears began to wash down her face. She stood up, spun in a circle, unsure of what she wanted to do. The rational part of her brain told her to walk out but the devastated part wanted to kill Anika and slug him right in the jaw so he would feel how much pain he caused. Juggling both thoughts, she turned and whispered, "Do you still love me?"

Peter got up from his chair and slowly approached her, afraid she would reject him. His eyes locked on hers and he choked, "I love you dearly. I have loved you my whole life. It happened so fast. I was out of my mind and out of control. I don't know what I was thinking. I never wanted to hurt you!" Peter opened his arms and hands and took another step.

Tears ran down Sarah's face, her anger and hurt clearly visible. "After all these years of love and friendship, you throw it all away! What can you possibly see in her? She is a bitch!" She stomped into the kitchen, slammed down the pans on the stove and sobbed.

Peter hesitantly followed the sound of her sobs. His mind was racing. *"What the hell did I do? What can I possibly do to recover this mess? I have to find a way to make her forgive me!"* He walked up behind her and lightly put his hands on her hips. She took a step away, then stopped. She stiffened. He slowly brought her hips closer to his and hugged her as she stood against the kitchen sink.

"Peter, no. no."

He stopped himself. A crackling silence filled the room. Peter ventured another step toward Sarah and dared to put his head on top of her shoulder. She didn't say anything. Sarah's body remained on guard, but she imperceptibly yielded, didn't resist. Peter started to cry. His sinuses were filling and with a raspy whisper he said, "I really am so sorry. I am stupid and I know I hurt you."

Sarah's body was tense, quivering with rage, fear, and despair. She wept into her hands as time stood still. Peter's tears ran off his cheeks onto her neck. He knew to keep holding Sarah firmly. Her tension eased a bit, then lessened more.

"Can you ever forgive me? I need you and I want to fix this. Please."

No reply.

Eventually, both drained from the emotions of the night, they went up to their room. They lay in the same bed but it felt as if the entire Arctic Ocean was between them. Facing away from each other, two strangers shipwrecked and grappling with their own thoughts. Nothing was said aloud, but the voices in their heads were screaming, a frightening clamor of confusion and sadness.

The next day, Peter arrived at the office emotionally and physically exhausted. When the receptionist called to inform him the attorney had arrived, he got up slowly to meet his friend in the lobby with his mind racing. *I am not sure I can get through this again. Hell, I don't even know if Sarah will ever forgive me and now I have to divulge this whole mess to Howard! I am so stupid!*

He greeted Howard and walked with him through the sea of cubicles. When they encountered Nicole, Peter asked her to join them in his office.

Peter's door closed. Before he could say a word, Howard slapped him on the shoulder. "Of all the things we have done together, you have done the stupidest and most irresponsible thing ever! How could you have a relationship with your staff? How could you hurt Sarah? This definitely beats out the time when we were teenagers and broke into Ms. Weaver's room." Howard looked at Nicole and explained, "We found Ms. Weaver's black grade book, then changed our homework and quiz grades from C's to

A's with a couple B's. Now, that was stupid." Looking back at Peter who was now sitting slumped at his desk, he continued to rant. "But THIS! Have you lost your mind?"

Peter was too depressed to rehash childish mistakes. Clearly, Howard had been brought up to speed; well, at least he didn't have to go through the whole story again. Looking to the ceiling, he thought, *"Thank you Nicole for saving me from that ordeal!"* Breaking out of his troubled mind, he snorted and acknowledged, "That was definitely stupid but doesn't even come close to this screw up. I feel so guilty! I honestly didn't know what was happening and I feel so ashamed. How could I have been such an idiot?"

Howard reached into his briefcase and handed two manila folders to Peter. Peter grabbed the folders but jumped up and shook his hand violently, which scattered the papers all over his desk. "Damn it! I just got a paper cut."

Shaking her head at him, she retorted, "You are going to get more than a cut if you don't take this seriously. You should be ashamed. I am upset as well."

Howard and Nicole collated the papers and put them back into their respective folders as Howard hesitantly asked, "How has Sarah taken this?"

"Obviously, she is extremely hurt and angry. I am pretty sure she will be for quite a while. Our marriage is so fragile right now! I can't lose her. I don't know what I would do if she left. I am trying to be positive though. I still think we will work it out. At least I hope so. I have to do everything I can to make this up to her." Peter rubbed at his eyes before anyone could see him tear up.

Nicole gave him half a smile. "She is the best thing that happened to you. If you screw this up, both of us will kill you. I mean it."

Howard took an audible deep breath. "I have prepared our next steps. We all need to agree and be on the same page every step of the way. If this backfires, it could crush and devastate Pure Air and have a greater impact on your marriage. Agreed?"

Nicole and Peter nodded their agreement.

Bob and Kevin saw Howard and Nicole walk into Peter's office. Kevin worried out loud. "This is not good news for us. I think today is the day they fire us."

Bob blew out a slow breath. "When I told you about Peter firing us, I didn't think it would be so soon. I have to say, I am a little nervous."

"I thought the promotions and the restructuring would give me some security."

"Me too."

"Should I start packing my stuff?"

Bob rubbed his hands together and ended in a near-praying position. "No, just wait. Let's see what happens."

Several other staff also saw Howard and Nicole follow Peter into his office. The grapevine instantly buzzed to life, including the remote workers; all speculating what the dire omens meant. Various rumors quickly gained ground. One was that Peter was retiring and Anika was going to take his place. Another rumor was that the sales office was going to be shut down and move to the factory. None of the rumors were encouraging news for the staff.

Nicole called Anika and asked her to come to Peter's office. She couldn't help wondering, *"Why is Nicole wanting me to meet her and Peter in his office?"*

When she walked into Peter's office she was stunned to see Howard there, too. Trying to shake the nerves that suddenly washed over her, she walked over to Howard and shook his hand.

Howard was extremely formal. "Good morning. Please have a seat. We have a serious situation to discuss with you, so I will get straight to the point. I think it is in everyone's best interest for you to tender your resignation effective immediately. We are offering three months' severance."

Anika eyes bulged. She gaped at all of them in the room. She opened her mouth to say something, but she was speechless.

"Here are two folders. One is for you and one is for our records. The top document in each folder is your resignation letter and needs to be signed right now. The second page is an acknowledgment of you receiving these documents. The rest of the documents describe the severance details." Howard handed Anika the two folders.

Instinctively, she grabbed the folders, opened one, and quickly scanned several pages. She looked incredulously at Peter after reading the first page, returned her attention to the second page, slowly lifted her gaze and glared at Howard then Nicole.

Unaffected by her stare, Howard assured her, "This is something we all agreed to. We hope to make this transaction as smoothly as possible." Placing a pen on the desk in front of her, he urged, "You can use this to sign the top document."

Overcoming her shock, Anika found her voice. "What the hell is this about?" She lifted her hand with the folders and slammed them down on the desk. "Are you trying to buy me off?" She looked at Howard.

When he didn't reply, she seethed, "Are you discriminating against me? I have done an incredible job here." Turning her ice cold eyes on Peter, she growled, "Oh, I know what this is about."

Nicole cut her off. "This has nothing to do with buying you off or about discrimination." Leaning forward in her seat, she made it clear to Anika she was not about to back down; she was ready to fight.

Avoiding Nicole's penetrating stare, Anika looked at Peter. "So, you told them what happened? You piece of –"

Howard interjected before she could finish her statement. "Hold on, let's talk through this. We don't need to yell."

"Don't tell me what I need to do. This pig over here took advantage of me." Anika pointed at Peter.

In that instant, Peter's confusion cleared and he saw the woman the way everyone else did...manipulative! He became angry...really angry. Without determining whether he was angrier at her or himself, he pointed his finger at Anika. "Listen here. I didn't want this and you kept on pushing and pushing and pushing."

"Don't tell me you didn't want it. We both know you willingly participated. Hell, it probably made you feel like a big man too!" Peter closed his eyes and shook his head.

Howard tried again, "Please, everyone, please! Let's be civil and talk through this."

Nicole jumped in with her calm, professional tone. "We can argue all day here. But that won't change anyone's mind. As Howard said earlier, there are two documents to review and sign." She pointed to the folders.

Anika flared back up. "You could have said no at any point, but you didn't. You wanted me to take the lead, you needed me to take the lead, admit it!"

Peter's anger subsided into pity and remorse. He leaned back, he wasn't going to fight her any longer, and just shook his head several times from side to side.

Nicole sensed Peter's demeanor change. But, her own anger remained. She looked at the folders once again. "Please. Just sign the documents."

Howard pushed the documents toward Anika. She looked at the documents and hissed, "I am not done yet!" Her eyes bore into Peter first, then she looked at Nicole.

"There is nothing more for us to say. Our offer stands," said Howard.

"I see that!" Anika looked at the folder as Howard slid it toward her. She thought, *"Should I sign then sue, or not sign and sue? What leverage do I have?"* She grabbed the folders and opened one to reread the letter.

Everyone was silent. Nicole and Howard's eyes were darting back and forth between each other and the folder. Peter's eyes had a glassy look as if he was in a stupor. Anika carefully read the resignation letter and the severance letter. She believed she was in the driver's seat and could dictate where to go next. She grabbed the pen.

Howard had much experience in these situations. He knew to control his breathing, keep his heart beat low, and remain calm. Nicole on the other hand had no poker face at all. She was angry, her breathing was noticeable, her heartbeat raced, and she squirmed in her seat while one of her legs jiggled on the floor. She desperately wanted Anika to sign those documents.

Anika tapped the pen on the resignation letter and smugly turned to Howard. "I am not sure I want to sign this now."

He looked at her and calmly said, "I recommend you sign the resignation letter now and acknowledge receipt of the severance package. You don't have to sign the severance letter today. You have seven days to sign and return." Howard knew she needed to sign within the next few seconds; otherwise, the documents would not be signed.

Peter was still in a trance. As Nicole unfolded her legs, Howard motioned toward Nicole like an orchestra conductor as if to say, "Stay there and be quiet."

In command of the room, Howard pointed to the top document. "Yes, that is the one you need to sign."

As Anika stood, Howard and Nicole took a deep breath and held it.

They watched intently as she slightly bent forward, clicked the pen, and signed the resignation letter, then signed the acknowledgment letter.

Howard breathed out slowly and thought, *"Victory! We did it."* Without belaying his thoughts, he encouraged, "Please sign the documents in the other folder too."

Nicole knew it wasn't over. She thought, *"If she touches me, I am going to scratch out her eyes."*

Howard organized one set of documents into a folder and gently handed it to Anika, then stood. "Thank you for signing. I can escort you to the reception area. For any personal items left at your office, we will box them and express courier them to your home."

"There is no need to escort me. I know the way to the front door, dammit." Anika tucked the folder into her purse, fiercely looked at Peter one last time and growled, "This is not over!"

Howard said, "We will need to have your smart key." He extended his hand to receive it, opened Peter's door and motioned for her to walk through it in front of him.

Anika did not want to be escorted. She aggressively handed Howard her badge and quickly walked through the lobby and out the front door. Howard followed her into the lobby and stopped at the front door. Nicole stayed behind in Peter's office.

The stunned receptionist hastily asked Howard, "What happened to Anika?"

"She no longer works here." He watched her walk into the parking lot, and when she was almost out of sight, he headed back inside.

Sarah arrived in the parking lot as Anika was walking out. When Anika spotted her she lifted her hand, then held out her middle finger as she continued walking. Sarah was shocked. She raised and pointed both her hands to Anika and gave her a five-second pity clap.

Anika mouthed a well-known sexual expletive and continued walking away from the building.

Sarah walked to the front door with an occasional glance in Anika's direction until she disappeared and thought with a smug smile, *I couldn't have timed it any better. I am so glad I could watch that witch leave!*

The receptionist smiled. "It's nice to see you Sarah. Guess who just got fired?"

"Yeah, I saw." Sarah kept walking.

The staff was perplexed. They rocked and shifted their heads back and forth looking for someone who might have an answer. Desperately looking for a leader who could tell them what to do and how to act.

Bob and Kevin witnessed Anika walk quickly out the front office followed by Howard. "I didn't see that one coming." Bob's grin was like a laser scanning the office.

"What? What just happened?" Kevin grabbed his armchair and readied himself to react.

"Well buddy, guess you won't need to pack any of your stuff today. We can decide the agenda for Monday."

"I don't get it. Wait. Do you mean Anika got fired?"

Bob stood up, raised his fists to the ceiling and swung them to the floor, and said, "Game over."

Still confused, Kevin repeated. "Game over?"

"Yeah, buddy. Anika is gone. Game is over."

Logan was emerging from a meeting, and he nearly walked into Howard. They gave each other a strange look as Howard closed Peter's door. Logan stood there looking at Howard, then saw Bob standing with his fists pointed to the ceiling. He headed in his direction thinking, "*Hmmm, wonder if he knows what's going on.*"

When he reached them, he heard some of the conversation. "What's going on?"

With glee, Bob informed him, "Anika just got fired."

"What? Really? Wow! I did not see that coming at all. Peter never said a word about that change."

Kevin cheered, "Hallelujah, the wicked witch is gone! Do you guys get that?"

Logan and Bob looked at each other and laughed.

Bob declared, "We are going out for beers! I am buying."

Howard disregarding all the whispering and confusion running rampant through the office and walked back into Peter's office.

"Are we done?" Peter asked with a sigh of relief.

"Not quite. We need to wait until Anika sends us the signed severance letter. If we receive it, then it is over. If we don't receive it, well, it may be a court battle."

"Well, if that bitch knows what's best, she will sign it. God, I hope she signs it."

Howard nodded but decided to remind him of one thing.

"You better hope she does. You certainly aren't completely innocent in all of this and you would do well to remember that!"

At that moment, Sarah walked into Peter's office, stunning everyone inside. Howard was first to speak. "Hi, Sarah. I am just about ready to leave. Thanks, Peter. We will talk soon. Bye, Sarah." Howard grabbed his briefcase and wanted to get out of the office as soon as possible. He didn't want to be involved in another fight, especially a spousal dispute.

Nicole reigned in the rest of her anger and brightly welcomed Sarah. "It's so nice to see you. How are things?"

"Well, to tell you the truth, I was upset driving over here. That changed once I saw Anika walk out the building. That bitch had the nerve to give ME the finger so I smiled at her and gave her a pity clap. That was my first smile in a while and it felt good."

Peter heard their exchange and on impulse, blurted out, "How about the three of us go out to eat?" The thought ran through his mind, *"Bringing Nicole would be a distraction and would lessen any anger Sarah still has. And, I could bring up Nicole's promotion and talk about all of us moving to the factory. This will work out well."*

Nicole gave Sarah a huge smile. "Sure. I think all of us could use some time away from here."

Sarah thought about it for a fraction of a second before she agreed. "Sounds just perfect."

www.ingramcontent.com/pod-product-compliance
Lightning Source LLC
Chambersburg PA
CBHW050733230626
47052CB00002BA/129